Our Lactating God

Our Lactating God

THE EMBODIED AMEN

Aubra Love

the pilgrim press

The Pilgrim Press, 1300 East 9th Street
Cleveland, Ohio 44114
thepilgrimpress.com

Published 2025.

Scripture quotations, unless otherwise noted, are from the King James Version of the Bible. Changes have been made for inclusivity. Printed on acid-free paper.

Library of Congress Cataloging-in-Publication Data on file.
LCCN: 2024949980

ISBN 978-0-8298-0112-5 (paper)
ISBN 978-0-8298-0113-2 (ebook)

Printed in The United States of America.

Contents

Introduction and Appreciation

I always expected that I would serve and build community in a parish that reflected elements of my childhood historic Black patriarchy. Oops, did I say "patriarchy"? Excuse me, I meant "church."

I was born roughly ninety years after the Emancipation Proclamation; not even a hundred years had passed since the end of the merciless institution of chattel slavery, of separating families and subjecting Black people to conditions worse than those of livestock. Ninety years is but a moment in the systemic cycles of oppression. It's one lifetime, a long life, but conceivably one lifetime. Not a very long time, at all.

In the church where I grew up, agricultural workers, factory machinists, homemakers, domestic service workers, teachers, and preachers took the Sabbath seriously as a day of rest. People who worked way too hard all week showed up for church in their finest attire to earnestly pray, sing their hearts out, wave their hands in praise, and rock as the Spirit moved. As naturally as rest follows labor, the staunchest workday enforcers and rigid gatekeepers would enter the sanctuary with such humility in countenance that they were difficult to recognize. One's influential post or lowly position in the community was laid aside for a few hours each week, where there were "no big I's and little you's." That was how our church put it. Everybody was on equal footing as we went before the throne of grace, because "God is no respecter of persons."

I learned to be enchanted by every minute of worship. The music in my family's church was live and jumping! The sermons were rhythmic, pointed, and filled with reconciling exhortation, commonly referred to as "call and response." The old folks hugged us children tightly, while kindly whispering admonitions for behavioral adjustments. "Baby, quit acting a fool. Trying to shame your mamma? You know better than that!" We knew they loved us and had noble expectations that soon we would run marathons with the batons of faith and justice, building on the strong foundation they diligently laid for us.

This is how we entered the "Lord's house": humble, expecting to receive something that could not be obtained elsewhere, something so mysteriously wonderful that it cannot be named. God, "which doeth great things and unsearchable; marvelous things without number" (Job 5:9 KJV). Reciprocally, pieces of that same "something" were extended among our neighbors and strangers throughout the week, making for a village of compassion and generosity. We ministered to each other in whatever ways were necessary, including a good cussing out if any of us were off track and on our way to hell. We reminded each other that "open rebuke is better than secret love" (Proverbs 27:5). I'll be damned if I am going to watch you on your way straight to hell in a handbasket. Rebuked with hugs and kisses, we called each other to account, back to good sense and godly ways.

Our church, founded a few years after the Emancipation, recently celebrated its 150th anniversary of safeguarding and ushering Black people through the transition from slavery to free citizenship in the United States of America. This transformative cultural experience is at the heart of every historic Black church, our primary nurturing institution. Black churches gave birth to historic Black colleges and missionary societies that were revolutionary in spirit, albeit discreet. The Greater Springfield Baptist Church—where I was baptized—at Jones Avenue and Griffin Street in Atlanta was so responsive to the lives of its membership and neighbors that occasionally, after the benediction, our very fine pastor the Reverend O.C. Woods would intone in his gravelly voice, "For those who can stay, Sister So-and-So and Brother Who's-It are going to unite in holy matrimony. Let us give them all the love we can, Springfield!"

Amen?

After a brief pause for children who needed a bathroom break and any diabetic who had to go eat, the organist—in full Little Richard vitality—would enthusiastically launch into a rendition of "Here Comes the Bride." Jazzy music like a New Orleans funeral, made especially for second-line dancing, would fill the sanctuary. The ring bearer, always a boy, would saunter down the center aisle; he'd be followed by a stream of swaying flower girls, sporting bouncy Shirley Temple curls and copper-colored Vaselined legs that "shone like new money" (new pennies), adorned with ruffled-anklet socks trimmed in white lace. Then the grand entrance of the bride in her full regalia: white dresses for brides who were virgins, pink satin-and-lace dresses for brides who were mothers.

Our pastor would deliver a little homily, offer blessings and a bit of stern counsel to the groom, before pronouncing the couple husband and wife. There was no budget for engraved invitations, musicians, caterers, limousines, or wedding coordinators. Our "school days" photographer was usually present and prepared to take a photo or two of the couple. And the church already had flowers from somebody's yard for worship, so nobody missed the florist too much. Oh, the colorful gladiolus! Also known as the African sword lily, gladiolus dressed the pulpit for three of four seasons in the warm Atlanta climate. My favorites were the white ones with a shock of deep purple in the center. The nuptials were witnessed and affirmed in the community of love and respect, and a new way of life began for the couple, with community blessings. Amen? A-a-amen!

"Chicken dinners for sale downstairs in the Fellowship Hall immediately following this service!" was broadcast over sanctuary loudspeakers. Paying for one's meal was all that was expected at the event, because any new wedding gifts were a group effort offered by the Springfield Heirs Adult Choir, the Social and Welcome Committee, or the Ladies Auxiliary. I sang in the Sunbeam Children's Choir, and I do not remember anybody ever wanting to dine with the wedding party who was not served a meal. "I have been young, and now am old; yet have I not seen the righteous forsaken, nor his seed begging bread" (Psalm 37:25).

As stated in John 21:12, "Come and dine" was the eleventh commandment in my family's church. Sister Thurmond was sure to have made one of her sweet potato pies, sometimes in lieu of a wedding cake. Those majestic brides would have upstaged any cake anyway, all day, every day! The brides, wearing pink satin and lace contrasted against the smoothest, blackest skin, were elegant, sweet, and stacked like life-sized chocolate wedding cakes themselves. Lord, have mercy!

The weddings and receptions were simply beautiful and spontaneous. This spontaneity eliminated any social self-doubt that comes with questions of, "Am I really invited? Do I know them well enough to show up? Will others think I just came to be nosy . . . or, even worse, for the fancy food and drink?" Everyone was heartily welcomed to celebrate this public declaration of love and the solemn promise to "stick and stay" together through whatever life may bring.

We were just a few generations from jump-the-broom weddings, where a commitment of love and fidelity between African-heritage people was not a matter of public record or even acknowledged beyond the family, church community, and local segregated neighborhoods. Way before cross-cultural marriages were commonplace in the United States—way before the topic of marriage equality would upset many a family gathering—our Black church community loved elaborately and lived simply. In that chasm of one hundred years from jumping the broom to casual cohabitation, these meaningful, holy, and sensual liturgies of love were lavish fellowship events in my church in Atlanta's Vine City neighborhood.

The Christian church is known as the Body of Christ, in part because our spiritual connection is a series of deeply ingrained bodily experiences. How do we encounter God? Often through our bodies. Through our shared community body. Through our singing and dancing, feeding and grieving. To the extent that the Body of Christ disconnects itself from the bodily experience, it disconnects itself from the authentic gatherings, honest relationships, and sincere nurturing that are needed. While the struggles of the church to catch up to the needs of the community are well researched and collective, this story is mine. I pray that you do not discount or dismiss it, preferring a more academic tone. I am talking directly to you, co-laborer!

Experiencing worship, embodied as Black and female, Southern and working class, demure and refined, educated, and with an often-made-up mind, I am sharing my experience of Jim Crow segregation, colorism in the Black community, and women's actualization reconciled with our African heritage, narrated against the tapestry which proclaims that our God is faithful. I offer this work as one more pathway to an intimate walk with our Divine power who is feminine, full of color, energetic and brimming with life-giving nourishment, music and dancing. My prayer is that this sharing—through story and song and food, just as we share together when we worship—can broaden our capacity and our power to bless God's people.

Come and go with me for the next glorious little bit of thinking and praying, rocking and preaching, dancing and cooking to the glory of God! We are the embodiment of God. Made in God's image. Let the redeemed shout, "It is so!"

I give thanks and high praise for my brilliant and beautiful, bouncing, brown babies, Alan and Tahira, and my adventurous granddaughter, Dylan, each of whom are always enthusiastic about my whole self. I am very proud and pleased to have shared more than 70% of my life with these accomplished, compassionate (adult) children whom every mother yearns for and our global society truly benefits from.

Beloved children, please always know that you are precious and loved beyond measure, a true extension of divinity!

Thanks be to our ever-generous God for my circle of supportive, ride-or-die, WTF sisters: "Wise, True and Fearless." I am thankful for my most treasured compatriots, my very best friend Patsy White, Organizer Extraordinaire, and my daughter in revolutionist thought Dia Hodnett, Global Health Strategist for Black and Indigenous Women.

I am abundantly blessed to dwell in the wholeness of the South Georgia healing flow of Patricia Sauls, in the clear and forward thinking of Laurie Dubrow, in the phenomenal organizing of Older Women by Thada Bornstein, in the First Tuesdays Convenings of Lauri Winter, in the Peacemaking among Jews and Gentiles of Joyce Ross, in the empathic advocacy on childhood poverty of Heléne Kass; to dwell as a witness to the "bridge" for Germans and Jews of Uta Allers, in the ray of the Sunshine (of my life) Ludwick, embraced by the manifold artistry of Mary "who used to be Mica," surrounded by the majestic vision of Ms. Gloria Chan and damn near everything about V. Renee Homes who still closely resembles the righteous Rock from which we are hewn (Isaiah 51:1). Thank you, brave women.

And in a category all her own, my daughter of the process and prophet of possibility, Dr. Cornelia Cho of Atlanta.

Finally, I want to acknowledge my faithful daughter of the process in this gospel ministry—and my iron sharpening iron for nearly 30 years—the Rev. Amanda Hendler Voss of Washington, DC.

There are a host of others who are very important to me, who encourage me, hold me up and send loving energy my way "on the regular." The good sisters at The Pilgrim Press, the Rev. Rachel Hackenberg and Kathryn (Katie) Martin, who walked with me through years of discernment and articulating this story in my most authentic voice. You are a gift to your cohorts! I am filled with gratitude for all the unearned blessings that are showered over me and are simply too numerous to name.

And certainly not least, I have boundless gratitude and limitless appreciation for every Adam who braved the garden of my Eve-energy to offer companionship, protection, provision, mutuality, humor, good sense and most of all, kindness. I am confident that the delicious apple, our fruit, brought wisdom and blessings of knowledge that were not heretofore ours. I pray a hedge of protection all around you, every day (Job 1:10).

To our Holy Maker who spans, yes surpasses, all mental and all emotional aspects of the human experience. The One, our lactating God, who feeds us and works through our bodies and beyond, with all spiritual sustenance. The embodied Amen.

Chapter One

Let's Talk about Rejection

Who among us has not known a stinging rejection that resulted in humiliation, self-doubt, and temporary or permanent ostracism? Church is called to be a balm for the dislocation caused by rejection, with Jesus as our triumphant example. Church is called to be a place of celebration of the unique nature of each sentient being.

As the fourth and final child of my parents, I weighed in at nearly fourteen pounds during a homebirth where my mother was given no anesthesia, only the comfort of low singing and moaning of midwives who understood that they were divinely called of God. There were no "colored" hospitals. There was no admission of "Negroes" to the segregated hospitals. I am reminded of early teachings I received on the birth narrative of Jesus, how my preschool-self struggled to comprehend legally enforced segregation, and to understand why there would be no hospital to care for my tax-paying mother and her incredibly painful childbirth process. I know she paid taxes because she said so. No room in the inn for some, for serious!

My birth narrative is filled with accounts of insufferable pain and overwhelm, as told and retold through the years by traumatized attendants and family, concluding with the punctuation that my parents ensured that my initials were A.L.L. They were done having babies, after me. We did not know back then that these oversized babies were the result of a mother's gestational diabetes. Babies, like me, with a birthweight over ten pounds were referred to as "fat and fine." The early rejection that I experienced as an infant was not related to birthweight—although this was a memorably painful, vaginal delivery for my mother.

The stories of my birth included a range of disappointments: Even though I was born to two Black parents, my eyes were not brown—and I was the third daughter in a succession of daughters. I was a big, fat, green-eyed baby girl. Our itinerant doctor and family friend, Dr. Albert Perry, only half-jokingly promised to develop a solution of silver nitrate to resolve this issue of eye color and ease my mother's anxiety. Interracial marriage was not legal in many states at the time. The punishment was extremely severe for racial "mixing," unless it was an act of coercive intercourse or violent rape perpetrated by a white man upon a woman of color. That's just the real. Real talk.

My brown-skinned, coffee-colored mother was afraid of the attention that such a huge, green-eyed baby girl would draw. She was afraid of the inferences that may be made about her own choices. My mother was the modest, first daughter among twelve siblings born to a pastor and schoolteacher, who lived a life of propriety. Even though I strongly resembled my father's side of the family, it was my mother who traveled about, sometimes on the bus with her baby girl, in a manner that brought intrusive questions about my paternity, racial identity, and legitimacy of birth.

Thank God, our "colored" itinerant physician's leadership as the president of the only armed, military-trained NAACP unit in the United States kept him too busy to perform his silver nitrate experiment with my eyes. Thank God for (nearly) perfect eyesight, on this day!

I was the third daughter when the ardent desire for a rough-and-tumble baby brother had to finally be put to rest. Having dashed all hopes of another son, I could feel resentment permeating throughout our household air. "Just please, not another girl." For these reasons, the spectacularism of the non-cesarean birth of a nearly fourteen-pound, green-eyed baby girl was fodder for many a conversation. It was talked about, often.

Babies are sensitive to negative energy. And I was acutely aware, even as an infant, that I was not the one who was anticipated, or longed for, in a system that made the adults anxious and hypervigilant. I grew accustomed to hiding my eyes, if possible, while seeking to connect. They said I was shy. Or as we say in the South, "shame-faceted" or bashful. I can own it. God still works through it, though. I knew that my green eyes would always be there, set prominently in my face; I was reminded by the pained looks and curled lips when I encountered others of my brown-eyed community.

Just a few years back, I was invited to visit with a church member in her home between the morning worship and a special evening program. Eager to make a new friend in this mature Black woman in our mostly white congregation, I quickly accepted her invitation. As I settled into her comfy sofa and soft pillows, she wanted to demonstrate her new Alexa virtual assistant, a Christmas gift from her son. My host, a Howard University grad in her eighties, asked Alexa, "What's a mulatto, Alexa?" Even this inanimate Christmas gift, Alexa, showed more thoughtfulness and hospitality than my prospective friend by responding, "I would rather not answer that question."

Thank you, Alexa, for not colluding with this assault of colorism and shaming! When I could not conceal my surprise and hurt from the insensitivity of her question, my tears began to roll. I am pretty healed up around this today, but on that day, I was still open from worship. This sister quickly admonished, "Oh, honey, my granddaughter is biracial. Sorry. Don't be so sensitive." I am so vulnerable and open after worship and preaching, that this tasteless gesture went in like a rusty dagger. Even as I write about it, the tears still burn. It is very old stuff . . . for both of us. She was in whatever her stuff was, too.

All those times—the emotional and physical violence that I experienced in my life because of how I looked—came rushing back in this old lady's house between church services: the people who stoked my mother's fear and discomfort about our difference in skin color; the insecure elementary school teachers who picked fights with me for no apparent reason; the older boy who violently raped me on my first date because I was "just like a white woman" but he "couldn't get in no trouble for it." Sexual assault was seldom prosecuted and not even taken seriously, with the exception of child victimization falling under certain statutory rape definitions. And it would take more than twenty-five years afterward, with organizing and agitation, to raise the age of consent in Georgia from fourteen to sixteen years old. I was hoping for a life that did not require political action after a childhood preoccupied with voting rights organizing. That's what I was hoping for.

There were the kids who taunted my kids about having a "light-skin-ded" mamma with "cat eyes," church leaders who questioned my authenticity about our shared ancestry, and my sincerity about a Black faith experience. No rest for the weary.

I was reminded of a female mid-career workplace superior whom I was determined to respect and support, at least to the level I had respected my white male C-suite colleagues in the financial industry over the years. In my position as a high-ranking comptroller in a national organization, I was answerable to her. This honcho-sister, as my direct supervisor, asked me to get her coffee during a morning meeting with out-of-town philanthropists and venture capitalists that she wished to impress. I was the chief financial officer, present to answer any questions about our organization's solvency.

Although I privately thought, "Why you trippin' today, sister?" I played along and got her the coffee. This was not among my duties. Everybody already knew that she was the "grand poobah" of women's organizing. When I returned with her coffee, she commented, "This ain't light enough." I froze in my attempt to understand her cues as she lowered her eyelids and whined rather obscenely, "I want it 'bout your color," while licking her lips and stroking her abdomen. This was the beginning of many boorish and demeaning sexual advances from her. Hear me clearly, this is not about gender identity, liberation, or free expression of sexuality. This is about sexual harassment, with economic implications.

This was before we had the clear feminist consciousness and legal precedents for sexual harassment in the workplace. My beloved Cornell University professor, Dr. Lin Farley, began her groundbreaking work by interviewing university co-eds about obstacles to summer employment. Our student interviews were published in her book, *Sexual Shakedown*, where she coined the term "sexual harassment," back in the 1970s.

It was my first time having an interview published. This was before the courageous Anita Hill testified against Clarence Thomas as a nominee for the Supreme Court. At that time, there was no legal recourse, empathy, or collective understanding about this abuse of power, its spiritual toll, and economic implications. We knew this never-talked-about epidemic spoiled employment opportunities for younger, unskilled women workers. Lo and behold, sexual harassment was alive and well in this "safe space" of a professional arena, nearly fifteen years after college graduation!

Colorism, no matter where it rears its ugly head, even in a sister's board room, is based in white racism against Black bodies. This is a painful critique no matter where one's skin color falls on the palette. Skin color and hypersexuality are often conflated because, in order to "make" this bouquet of skin colors, a forbidden sexuality becomes evident and must be acknowledged. It is not rational, yet it is so.

This could be a whole chapter on what we now understand about Kimberlé Crenshaw's pioneering analysis of intersectionality as the impact of interlocking systems of power which contribute to violence against women. Time spent here would lead us to a clearer understanding of how racism, misogyny, sexuality, classism, and multilayered marginalization contribute to political, structural, and economic violence against women, including domestic violence, rape, and underemployment. The church has the potential to be a place of action and healing in this regard as we learn to listen to and affirm the witness of our majority membership of women.

I learned early to not see myself. Later, I did the critical, personal work with the attention of many counselors, teachers, intimates, sponsors, and comrades, to learn that even though I did not appear to be who was longed for, in some situations, I was indeed enough—and I was often spectacular. Awesome, flat-out! Sorry, but the church was not much help with that.

Yes, I learned that I was more than enough and even sweeter than deserved. A few things are beyond my control, however, like gender, birthweight, eye color, skin color, and the pervasiveness of institutionalized racism and even internalized racism. With all this, it helps to remember that I am blameless in the eyes of God. This is true of you, too, just in case you need to hear it. You are loved, completely, by the One who is love.

Against conventional wisdom, my mother decided to breastfeed her oversized baby until I went to school, as immunity from childhood disease. It worked out. She confided that she only stopped breastfeeding because I began to argue with her in public when I wanted to be nursed, as a kindergartener, with a full set of teeth. Must have been awfully sweet stuff to create such a demanding posture in a shy, withdrawn five-year-old girl.

Dulce De Leche

MUSIC *Yes Lord, Yes* by Shirley Caesar

Do not be deterred if your first batch of Dulce de Leche (caramelized milk) is not so cute. It will still taste good if you don't let it burn.

INGREDIENTS

4 cups of milk
Just shy of 2 cups of sugar
Couple capfuls of vanilla

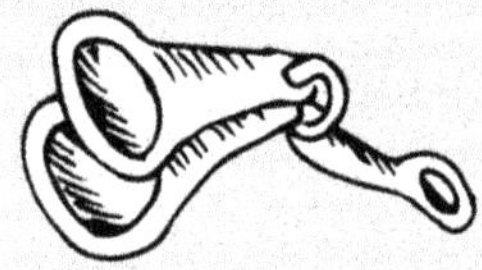

INSTRUCTIONS

Pour milk and sugar (2:1 ratio) into your best heavy bottom saucepan. Let it boil and reduce heat to simmer with no lid. Stir it up, until it gets thick or "caramelized." This will take about 1 hour and 45 minutes. At the 1-hour point, you will want to stir more often to keep it from burning.

Take it off the burner and drop in your vanilla extract. Pour mixture into a bowl to cool. Makes just shy of 2 cups and keeps well in a tight container. Great topping for brownies, cakes, ice cream . . . or by the spoonful.

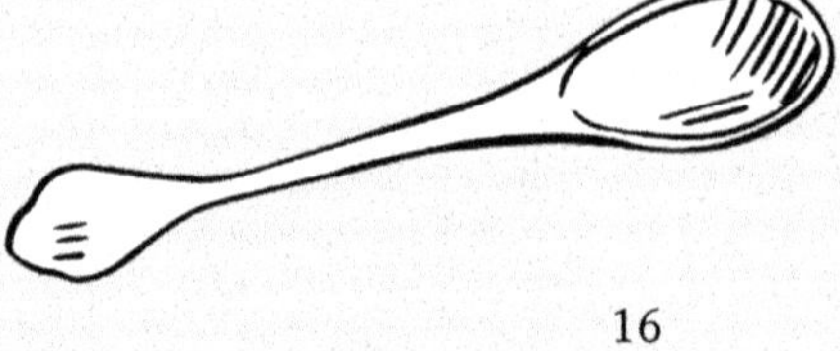

EASY SISTER RECIPE OPTION

INGREDIENTS

1 14 oz can sweetened condensed milk

INSTRUCTIONS

Remove label and any adhesives for a clean can. Fill crockpot with water. Place can in crockpot. Slow cook overnight. And you're done; no stirring! Yummy!

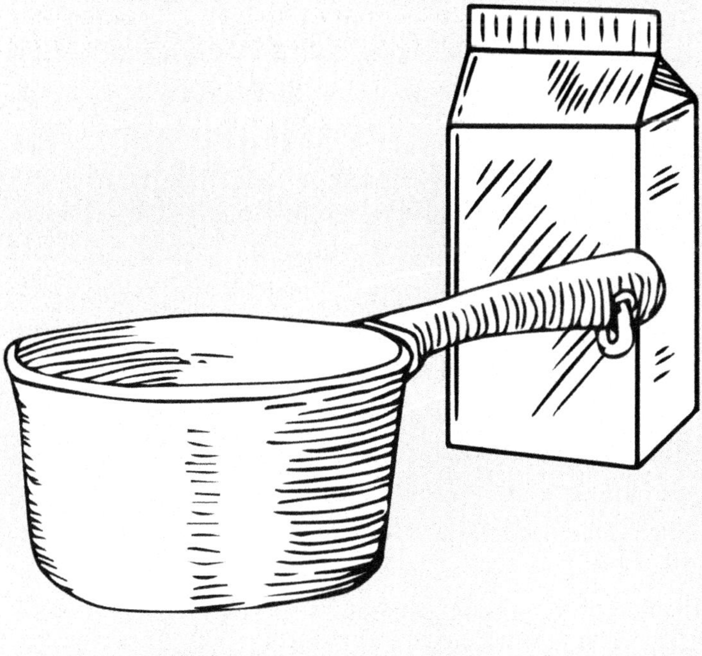

Chapter Two

The Awakening

Mrs. Odessa P. Davie ran things!

She wore stacked heels that made an intimidating noise when she walked, with such determination, on the tile floor in the hallway. Her hosiery was opaque; it was what we called "pe-can tan"—a bit too light for her complexion, but that was the style in the early 1960s for Black women who were professionals. Her hair was always neatly coiffed in a bob, or what we called a pageboy style. I was mesmerized by Mrs. Davie's hair! It was shiny and silver, with a hint of blue rinse that sometimes came out light purple. Her blue or purple curds of short fluffy hair reminded me of my mother's yard, full of purple and blue hydrangeas.

Mrs. Odessa P. Davie was my elementary school principal in the Jim Crow public school system of Atlanta. And, you better know, she ran things. Most faculty and students, maintenance and cafeteria workers—they all thought Mrs. Odessa P. Davie was an iron lady. My mother, a teacher in Atlanta public schools, taught us to respect Mrs. Davie's austere presence. By the time I started elementary school,

Mrs. Davie already knew my family and my older siblings. Because of this, she insisted on excellence from me.

During third grade, I was sent to her office because I was too quiet; I had been silent all day long. In the 1960s, that was considered a disciplinary problem. Now, we call it "meditation." But Mrs. Davie sat at her oversized metal desk, engaging me with questions about my future. On the wall behind her army-surplus desk was a reproduction of Van Gogh's famous painting, "Sunflowers." This sparked my interest in Vincent Van Gogh, and I later learned that he was called to ministry and went to seminary a bit.

Mrs. Davie began many of her sentences with, "Our children." Like, "Our children" this or "Our children" that. We knew somehow that "Our children" meant "Our Black children." It meant, "You, beloved, young folk." It meant, "All y'all precious little babies who bear the cultural burden of being the prayerful, moral compass of our country." We knew what she meant because every day we solemnly recited the Pledge of Allegiance to our flag: "One nation, under God, indivisible, with liberty and justice for all." Then we sang "For the Beauty of the Earth" or "Jesus Loves the Little Children"—you know, "all the children of the world." After singing our devotional song, we closed this daily communion with the Lord's Prayer.

One day in late November, just before the school session broke for the Thanksgiving holidays, Mrs. Davie ran out waving her arms in a jerky, uncontrollable fashion which signaled that she had lost all her usual composure. She yelled in a most undignified voice, a voice no proper lady would have spoken in ... not in the early 1960s. To see Mrs. Davie's lack of control, trembling and yelling, we thought the school building might be on fire; some of you may recall that we had frequent fire drills during the traumatizing 1960s, seemingly every other day.

We ran to Mrs. Davie from the far end of the playground. When we were within arm's reach, she grabbed as many of us as she could possibly hold. And the rest of us grabbed ahold of each other, as Mrs. Davie cried out, "Children, children we must go inside. The President has been shot!" The Birmingham bombing of schoolgirls in church, our same age, was only a couple months earlier.

We huddled up in the school auditorium to watch the news coverage on the boxy black and white television on the big rolling cart. And we held onto each other and wept. We had all been together when Mrs. Davie moved the picture of our former President, General Dwight David Eisenhower, to make room for the black-and-white photo of our young, handsome President John F. Kennedy. We had learned together that the Kennedy family listened, as true allies, to the demands of the Civil Rights Movement. We knew the Kennedys were for "our children" living and thriving in a just world.

Bobby Kennedy was the Attorney General at the time, undergirding his brother John's administration as leader of the "free world." They worked to end discriminatory practices in school admission policies, public school lunch programs, and the misallocation of resource materials and textbooks. You see, the Kennedy brothers had seen the defaced textbooks that were distributed to "our children," the mutilated textbooks that bore the unfamiliar names of other people's children and hand-drawn cartoons of Black children with bones through their noses and ethnic slurs inscribed. The Kennedys had seen the rationing of food to "our children," depriving them of the meal that was supposed to be served in every public school. For some, the meal served within the school lunch program was the only daily meal the child was provided.

Even more than that, the Kennedys were people of faith who understood in the 1960s that faith communities were key organizing institutions in justice-making for life, liberty, and the pursuit of happiness. The brothers were, by no means, perfect people, but they believed that political leaders and citizens were coalescing to end the Jim Crow practices in the U.S.: "one nation, under God, indivisible, with liberty and justice for all." President John F. Kennedy believed in this enough to ride through downtown Dallas, TX in a motorcade, while seated in an open convertible.

In his inaugural address in 1961, President Kennedy said: "Let both sides join in creating a new endeavor ... where the strong are just and the weak secure and the peace preserved. All this will not be finished in the first one hundred days. Nor will it be finished in the first one thousand days, nor in the life of this administration, nor even perhaps in our lifetime on this planet. But let us begin."

Grieving together in the elementary school auditorium in 1963, Mrs. Davie told us that "our children" must prepare themselves to take their rightful place and make our country better. "Lead the way with hard work, good educations, and staying close to Jesus," Mrs. Davie said. "You must be very sure that you study your lessons and stay in prayer." She closed her post-assassination counsel to us with, "You see what folk will do to their own, who want to end segregation. You're going to need your education. And you're going to need the Good Lord."

"Don't take any of this for granted," St. Paul wrote to the Church in Ephesus. "Christ came and preached peace to you outsiders and peace to us insiders. He treated us as equals, and so made us equals. God is building a home. God is using us all—regardless of how we got here—in what is being built. We see it taking shape day after day—a holy temple built by God, all of us built into it, a temple in which God is quite at home." (Ephesians 2:11 and 17–22 excerpted, MSG)

The call to action? People of God, lean in and listen up! What kind of church are we becoming for all our children? God is building a home, brick by brick, and everyone is included.

May peace be upon the souls of Patrice Lumumba (assassinated January 17, 1961); Addie Mae Collins, Denise McNair, Carole Robertson, and Cynthia Wesley (assassinated in the bombing of the 16th Street Baptist Church of Birmingham, September 15, 1963); John Fitzgerald Kennedy (assassinated November 22, 1963); Malcolm X (assassinated February 21, 1965); Martin Luther King, Jr. (assassinated April 4, 1968); Robert Francis Kennedy (assassinated June 6, 1968).

Cathead Biscuits

BODY BREAK

MUSIC *What You Gonna Do When the World's on Fire?*
Birmingham Jubilee Singers

INGREDIENTS

4 cups self-rising flour
1 pinch salt, optional
3 tbsp bacon drippings (or shortening), as desired
1¾ cups buttermilk, or clabbered milk
¼ cup butter, melted, for brushing, or for added flavor

INSTRUCTIONS

Preheat an oven to 475 degrees F. Grease an 8-inch cake pan. Sift flour and salt together into a large mixing bowl. Make a dent in flour by pushing flour from the center toward the sides of the bowl. Add 3 tablespoons of bacon drippings and a little buttermilk to the flour where the dent is made. Work the bacon drippings into the flour using fingers in a twisting motion until the drippings are completely mixed into the flour. Pour buttermilk (or clabbered milk) into the flour about ¼ cup at a time, continuing to work it in using fingers until the buttermilk is absorbed into a sticky dough.

Roll dough into 8 tennis-ball sized "catheads" and place into prepared cake pan, around the sides adding the last one in the center of the pan. Press "catheads" with the back of your fingers to flatten them into touching each other. They should be flattened to about ¾ to 1-inch thick.

Bake in preheated oven for 18 minutes for most ovens, or until the tops are golden brown. Brush tops with melted butter. Serve 'em up!

Chapter Three

When I Was Thirteen

Indulge me as I declare that thirteen is my lucky number. At thirteen years old, I could sing like Etta James; "I'd Rather Go Blind" was a favorite. Mamma called that "broke-down" music and admonished me for singing it, which made it irresistible.

Honey, thirteen is my lucky number. At age thirteen, I could ride all the way to downtown Atlanta on those old, mechanically unsound buses, right over to my junior high school. This was before MARTA in Atlanta. That's the Metropolitan Atlanta Rapid Transit Authority; legend has held that MARTA is an acronym for "Moving Africans Rapidly Through Atlanta." It's an old joke that offends some people. Atlanta is truly a very Black city if you haven't noticed.

When I was thirteen, I got a twenty-five-cent raise at my job, when minimum wage was $1.60 an hour. In the daytime, I was allowed to visit my fourteen-year-old boyfriend who was a caddie at East Lake Country Club.

When I was thirteen and had given my life to Christ the previous summer, my church had confidence in me enough to support me preparing twelve-year-olds for the baptismal rites. That's when I really got to know Jesus. By the age of thirteen, I was gifted with the ability to call up a rally, if necessary.

Back in the day, revolutionists like us had teach-ins, and by the age of thirteen, I could participate in a more active way! Teach-ins helped our community unify in ideology, strategies, social policies and priorities. It was critical that each organizer knew the people who may be in their immediate area during a demonstration, protest, or civil unrest. We needed to know our comrades. God forbid, you were tear-gassed, beaten or hosed—you needed to know who would cover you. Teach-ins made community in a way that social media cannot. Our social media platforms go wider, but community teach-ins helped the people unify through a specific, tangible understanding of deeply rooted class stratification, the feminization of poverty, and the systemic abuse of power.

At thirteen, I could make all my own clothes from patterns I designed for myself on newspapers, then cut out. And because I got off work after the second shift, I could talk on the phone all night long without interruption.

Thirteen was my age of wisdom, wise as a serpent, harmless as a dove. In some ways, being thirteen could be described as a "snake age," because I was wise, lithe, adaptable, and always renewing by shedding the old skin when it became too tight and no longer served a righteous purpose. I was unpretentious. Harmless, like a little garter snake, but my mouth was open so wide it covered my entire face . . . the way a snake opens her mouth. A powerful, untamed, sanctified snake, just muscle and motion. Just muscle and movement. No regrets! When I was thirteen.

When I was thirteen, it was the first realization of my approaching womanhood. I wore a bra for the first time, experienced my first menstrual cycle, and more importantly to me—at that time—it was the first time I was distinguished from the boys. Before, we had all been pretty much the same, but suddenly, I was treated differently, looked at differently, talked to differently.

Thirteen was the first taste of what my adulthood might be like. And for a child that young, on the verge of so many things, community is necessary. It is an excellent time for the church to be that community.

So much sexual objectification can happen during puberty. The church can intentionally affirm that thirteen-year-olds are simply people, developing, who still have the minds of children. Our young folk need protection. And what greater call can there be for the church than to protect the innocent?

Because I was raised in the historic Black (Baptist) church, all the way back to the boat, I was dyed-in-the-wool. That is to say, the traditions of my faith go culturally back all the way to when our people arrived in North America. I was deeply entrenched in Baptist dogma, belief, and practice as were so many African-heritage descendants of slavery on this soil. Some of that dogma, belief, and practice included a Jesus who especially loved us, as a people. A Jesus whose compassion was, first, for us. Then, if any compassion was left over, others could have some . . . perhaps.

Between the ages of twelve and sixteen, I was working. I went to school from seven in the morning 'til two thirty in the afternoon, and then worked an eight-hour waitressing shift until eleven at night. After work, my mother would let me sit on my front porch with my boyfriend, who had a similar schedule. The rigidity of our days, all of that working and barely squeezing in any time to be human—it was almost like being incarcerated. But I wasn't unhappy; this was how life looked for everyone in my proximity. I thought this was normal.

My big brother always worked, so I thought he was an adult. He was only eight years older than I, but his life was so full. He always went to camp, hung out in the afternoons at the Boys Club at the Butler Street YMCA in Atlanta, and was a lifeguard at the segregated public pools. He brought home every ailing animal and nursed them back to health. I actually called him "my big brother" when addressing him.

My sweet big brother went to Camp Allatoona one summer and delegated his jobs to his baby sisters. He did this for two reasons: First, we, his sisters, could keep his jobs for him until he returned from camp and would need to earn money to buy his school clothes; and second, we could use our earnings to buy fabric and make our own school clothes.

One of his jobs was to rise at dawn and go sweep the parking lot at Barker's Corner Store before it opened. My sister and I enjoyed getting out early before the hustle and bustle of the city began. We chuckled with each other that we were out and about each morning when it was still "blue" outside. We handled this responsibility well together.

Another job was cleaning all the fish that Mr. Raymond, our neighbor, caught and dropped off on our back porch in an ice-bucket-style cooler. We knew absolutely nothing about cleaning fish, but we made a noble attempt. Scales, everywhere. Fins, flying off the knife. Eyes gouged out. Our final masterpiece consisted of a bony skeleton with a few shreds of pinkish flesh and a couple of small internal organs . . . but mostly bones. Mr. Raymond expressed his grief that we had destroyed his catch and his week's portion for meals. My mother would not allow him to pay us and even sent him meals each day that week.

As time soothed his disappointment, and my big brother returned from camp, Mr. Raymond kidded my big brother that he must have been drunk or angry to mutilate the fish in that way. We found this hilarious because my Nation of Islam-adherent big brother never drank or displayed a vengeful spirit. My big brother was a devout and disciplined Muslim as far back as I can remember. Even though our family was Baptist, there was no tension about my big brother's faith because we were all poor, all oppressed, and all Black in our community. At the time, the brothers in "the Nation" all wore suits and were kind and disciplined Black men. Aside from this, the Black Baptist church was the only place where Black men could actualize as CEOs and own corporate real estate—church buildings and campuses—so we embraced all Black faith communities and entrepreneurship, whether Christian, Muslim, or Black Hebrew Israelites.

In the midst of all that heaviness, rigor, and oppression, we found happiness. But something needed to change. Being a Black Baptist meant fully embracing, without evaluation or scrutiny, the hermeneutic that was presented in our churches. My primary relationships were homogenous—with other Black people—mostly due to Jim Crow laws that harshly enforced a segregated South in all public institutions and facilities. I worked hard in high school and, at the age of sixteen, my commitment to academic and moral discipline was rewarded by an academic scholarship to Cornell University in Ithaca, New York. Affirmative action was making a critical difference for qualified students who were subjected to oppressive college admission practices, denying them access to higher education. I was always on the dean's list!

Strawberry Salsa

BODY BREAK

MUSIC *In the Garden* by Marvin Sapp

INGREDIENTS

16-ounce container fresh strawberries
1 jalapeño, diced
1 small red onion, diced
large mint leaves, chiffonade (fancy word for super-thin ribbons)
1 lime, juiced
1 tablespoon honey
1 teaspoon salt

INSTRUCTIONS

Remove stems from each strawberry and cut strawberries into small pieces. Combine all ingredients in a bowl and toss until well combined and lime juice and honey are evenly distributed. Serve immediately, or chill before serving. Store salsa in an airtight container in the refrigerator for three to four days.

Chapter Four

God's Lactating Promise

As a "no-time-to-waste" twenty-year-old, I had already completed my undergraduate education at Cornell University, married my college sweetheart Rutherford, and given birth to our beautiful and "asked for" son. It was a joyful time, even as my young husband and I struggled to embrace the challenges of physiological, mental, and spiritual upheaval that seemed to cycle through almost quarterly. We lost our minds every sixty to ninety days, still growing up in fits and starts. We could not always remember what direction we intended to head toward in life. We were in love.

There were gaps in our compatibility, but we were among a smattering of Black students in a sea of about twenty thousand white students at our large, impersonal, though well-respected Ivy League institution. We shared a library carrel. He worked in the stacks to supplement his scholarship for tuition and fees. I was a host announcer (or disc jockey) at WVBR-FM, the university radio station:

Take a journey into the inner depths of your soul. Let your mind and body flow freely, as one, while you relax to the sounds of Stevie Wonder, War, or The Delfonics, and Major Harris serenading you with "Love Won't Let Me Wait." Quench your thirst for musical entertainment and let us show you the beauty of ecstasy. Join the music odyssey with none other than the Sounds of Blackness on WVBR-FM. This hour brought to you by Turback's of Ithaca.

This was my Lady Love sign on.

Rutherford and I comforted each other, holding on tightly while we treaded water together. We managed to stay afloat. We were certain this was enough to make a lifelong marital commitment. With maturity, it became clearer that it wasn't.

Our financial resources were nonexistent. And our relatives tried repeatedly to "borrow" our scholarship funds for their own subsistence and chronic indebtedness. Our love was deeply loyal, passionate, unencumbered, and foolishly simplistic. We were the best of friends in a lockstep life of academic achievement, political engagement, discovery of boundless adult responsibility, and unbridled play. Lots of play. We were teenage friends in love who married and became parents. But we were still kids ourselves, so it was an erratic kind of life, bouncing between being adults and children.

One day, after too many days in the house caring for our newborn, I resorted to drastic tactics. Feeling uninteresting, I decided I might enjoy having a humongous, platinum-blonde afro. We called that style a "cotton-top 'fro." I bleached my natural, soft jet-black, virgin hair into a red-orange straw mat. My hair would not "blonde" after multiple chemical assaults. Just would not cooperate. Horrified and a little embarrassed by the result, I cried all night.

Of course, with our newborn son, I didn't sleep much anyway. I didn't know a person could go days on end without sleeping. Yet every reality check that I looked for in my most trusted friends was met with commentary attempting to normalize the experience. One of my closest friends from high school had the nerve to swear that giving birth was not a painful experience. I later learned that she was not conscious when her son was born. Sometime between when she gave birth, three years before me, and when I gave birth, the standard protocol for childbirth had evolved from gas that allows a birthing mother to sleep to natural childbirth with coaches urging the mother to "Push!" It was the hardest work I have ever endured. That same high school friend encouraged me to do it again "because it only hurts the first time." Gullible me!

I am more than grateful for my children and childbirth experiences. Frequently, through great pain comes the sweetest joy. Way after a while, I understood that. But not as a twenty-year-old. Living off mostly Chips Ahoy! cookies and quarts of whole milk, I was not sure if anyone understood how hard becoming a mother was for me. I was accustomed to being outside and moving around all day if the weather was favorable, as it was year-round in Atlanta; our place was spacious and tidy, but I felt caged and cut off. As the baby of my big, Southern family, I had never spent much time around a newborn, so I had no idea about all that was involved. I felt woefully inadequate and forgotten about. Jesus! Lamb of God, I come!

Observing my fits of sitting in the dark in silence and of endless weeping, my sweet, young husband asked what he could do to reengage me in family life. I quickly requested that he walk me down to the neighborhood Woolworth's store to buy a television set. Maybe the TV could distract me for a few years, and we could get through this childrearing thing. Then, I could get back to him, maybe, and we could enjoy our sweet child and family life. I needed a little emotional distance, or so I thought. Too many feelings. He did not hesitate, grabbing his windbreaker, we were out the door.

I was so fascinated to be out in the world again! In those days, before HMOs and the overt politicization of affordable healthcare, new mothers were cared for in the hospital for a week or even longer. This care was followed by thirty days of staying at home, except for church attendance. Having worked real jobs since I was eleven years old, I found this sitting at home quite boring and could imagine that our infant was also climbing the walls from lack of stimulation. While Rutherford and I ran out the door, our baby was well-fed and put down for a nap under my visiting mother's watchful eye. Thank you, Jesus, we had escaped to the downtown Woolworths in Ithaca, New York!

The store was only a couple of blocks away. I felt as if I was at a Caribbean carnival once I got there. All the bright retail colors, sounds, sights and smells, laughter and chatting. Only things missing were celebrating, dancing Black folk in dashikis, and the carnival stilt-walkers in colorful streamers! First time out in a while. Awakening all my senses, I was simply loving being out with my fine, hot-chocolate, long-legged, track-running husband with the "peas-y" hairs on his chest, just like the years before we were parents—until I heard a screeching infant. It was a hungry cry that would not be denied.

I was disturbed by this wretched call for comfort. I am pretty sure this was not a Black child, let alone a Southern baby, unlikely a baby girl living in poverty. After all she was with someone in this retail store, famous for racial discrimination, in the middle of the afternoon. For sure, this was not my baby. But somehow, I could relate. No, it was a little more than "relate." Listen, my breasts filled with a heaviness I had never known, followed by a tingling sensation and a burst of maternal energy. I needed to fix that situation with that baby. (Hungry Baby Alert in aisle four and blue lights flashing in my head!) My blouse was blotted with big oily circles as the creamy liquid ran down my stomach. First, I was alarmed, then euphoric from lack of sleep, then totally confused.

My husband was amused that my body could do all this. We had been together for four years, married for two years, taken prenatal classes together, read all the T. Berry Brazelton stuff, and learned Lamaze strategies for childbirth. But this unimaginable milk-on-demand reflex for a stranger's baby must have been covered in that Lamaze class we skipped to go to the movies. We were not prepared for this milk letdown response!

My husband wrapped me in his windbreaker jacket, his curious smile on his face—the one that caused his forehead to wrinkle in multiple handsome, meaty creases. With all my senses open and pulsating on high alert, in that moment—hyperarousal, I think it's called—I fiercely wanted six babies with this truly decent, trustworthy man. I can't really describe it; I wanted something more intensely than I could apprehend. However, I had already learned growing up to console myself when I had to choose my own wellbeing over any demanding, irrational impulse. "Wantin' ain't gettin'!" and "people in hell want ice water" were chiding refrains I learned for wanting something that was not within reason for the specific situation. It just wasn't to be together-for-life, with me and Rutherford. I might have to get over it.

We were doing all right for two kids who finished at the top of our high school classes and who were still in bad need of parenting. We made all our decisions jointly. More like, he made all our decisions. I was cool with that, though. Rutherford made sure I voted wisely. He was very interested in my safe, affordable birth control options. He made sure I had a valid driver's license, registration, and liability insurance. He opened my bank account to hold my scholarship funds and work-study money. He taught me how to use the bank, though I was not that interested. He even patiently instructed me on his method for taking notes in class lectures; though I had a photographic memory, his note-taking method mattered at exam time. He made sound decisions. I cooperated and loved him, blindly. And it was working out.

But, this milk, on that day, just decided to flow all on its own. No conversation. Didn't seek permission or agreement from anybody. While walking back home with our new thirteen-inch black-and-white television set, it was apparent that I was different, and that obviously, I was an entity that could never be totally controlled. How was that ever going to work? The mysteries of life after puberty continued to unfold in Rutherford's company over the next several years. I loved growing up with him. Grateful for all the firsts that we shared. But after that involuntary milk letdown, I began to think about more profound matters.

I didn't play as much. I was disturbed by the realization that all the divisions of humankind are learned, indoctrinated, and enforced in the harshest of ways. When it comes to church-folk wanting to build the inclusive community, it is no wonder we don't believe that we can. We do not believe that we can learn quickly enough to access our God-given power to truly connect across difference. Yet, outside of our human distress and systems of devaluation, God cries out, "I've got what you thirst and hunger for, for your long-term survival. I do not keep it on different shelves, or in separate, specially marked waiting rooms . . . like 'colored' and 'white.' I AM your step-right-up source." That is a holy "come and get it" if I ever heard one!

On that unseasonably chilly day in late August, I was completely taken by a tender madness that stimulated an indescribable desire in me to find and feed that hungry baby in this Woolworth's, where I had never seen a person of color—employee or patron. Without regard for the institutional hatred and the infamous retail character of Woolworth's stores, I knew that there was a hungry, distressed person in my vicinity and that I was the one, in that moment, who could be the resolving vessel.

As a woman who holds cultural memory of Woolworths as the place of lunch-counter demonstrations during our country's legally enforced segregated public dining, I marvel that I could even release breastmilk in this setting of invulnerability. This was my first time in Ithaca's Woolworth's; I had not patronized the racially segregated Woolworth's stores since childhood because of their very public reputation of active racial discrimination in rendering service. Yet in my postpartum state, my whole being urged me to seek out the hungry infant as I held this tainted, racialized memory of the Woolworth's from my childhood. This contradiction entered my soul.

Despite this cultural history, my body responded to provide comfort, seeking to feed and sustain the infant, while my soul urgency interrupted that reality with my higher duty. My present duty was to get back to my own baby, who could be awake and hungry; to check on my visiting mother who had not cared for an infant in decades; and to not embarrass my husband of solid middle-class values by ferociously searching through the store and ripping open my blouse to answer the cry of this stranger-baby.

But, how about that, though? I had milk! Me? A child born of apartheid in the United States. Born at home because hospitals did not admit Black people. Educated in segregated schools with used, torn, and defaced textbooks. I had what was needed, right then. I had more than enough! It was overflowing for any new human being who sent out a distress signal. I had what was needed! It was not Black milk. It was not Southern milk. I did not have a specific minority milk, no gay or straight milk! This was not Jim Crow milk. Or Equal Rights milk. I did not have school-to-prison-pipeline milk or public-assistance milk. My milk was not exclusively for future felons, or victims of over-policing or educational and healthcare disparities. It was simply life-sustaining milk. I had milk for the world, springing effortlessly from my bosom! Effortlessly!

Me? A child of literacy activists who perilously labored in voter registration drives, I had everything essential for ending this present suffering of another human being . . . even if it was not socially acceptable and, in some places, thought to be illegal. God spoke through the prophet Isaiah: "Can a woman forget her suckling child, that she should not have compassion on the fruit of her womb?"

(Isa. 49:15). Can a nursing mother forget her infant? This question is followed by God's declaration that "yes, they may forget, but I will not forget you." This is the assurance that God offers in this passage through the prophet Isaiah to us.

You know, God is saying to us, "This is how I am about you. And even more so! Can a mother forget the child she is still nursing?" God not only asks this question, but God answers it. The response is one that promises to hunt us down in the vilest of places, ignore all socially constructed separation, and greet us with resolution and comfort. "Your mother might momentarily forget you, but the weeping of her breasts will remind her. I AM THAT I AM. And I will never forget you!" That is what God has promised to us. God reminds us by offering a "stretch-out" comfort in these words. Just like a breastfeeding mother experiences surges of hormones that make lactation possible.

In my God-consciousness, I came to realize that what I had was good for the survival of the people and the planet! Up until that point, I believed my milk letdown was specifically and uniquely for my own infant. I felt something somewhere between fear and exhilaration, confidence and deep humility. God had unexpectedly shown up amid my lockstep relationship with my husband. I felt reverence for my own feminine biology, to experience that there was a process at work in my life more intricate and powerful than I had ever known—and it was good and special, not in the small way that I had become accustomed to thinking, but in infinite ways that I could not even comprehend. I was relieved to surrender and not burst under my own pressure. I was forever changed! I knew with my whole being that I was a part of all humanity—with the ability to respond, to ease suffering, to calm fears, to strengthen, to reassure, and to comfort. This is how God is about us. I decided that life is vast and hopeful. I knew I was an essential piece of *that*!

I am reminded of this story of my first milk letdown response whenever I read the scripture about our lactating God in Isaiah 49. This experience taught me, at twenty years old, that I was an integral part of the Holy and that caring is inherent; compassion extends beyond my immediate relations, beyond my circle of youthful friends, and beyond persons of a particular demographic, identity, or life experience. I was part of it all. Integral to the full scope of humanity. Now, run and tell that!

Pretty Pomegranate Feta Salad

BODY BREAK

MUSIC *Reckless Love* by Cory Asbury

INGREDIENTS

10-ounce package mixed baby greens
1 pomegranate, peeled, seeds separated
1 small red onion, finely sliced
½ cup pecan halves (candied if you are fancy and have a sweet tooth)
1 package feta cheese
Teeny bit of Dijon mustard
Shot of red wine vinegar
Shot of extra-virgin olive oil
Lemon, room temperature for juiciness

INSTRUCTIONS

Put mixed baby greens, sliced red onion, pecan halves, pomegranate seeds, and feta cheese in a big mixing bowl. In a separate bowl, whisk together Dijon mustard, vinegar, olive oil, and lemon juice. Pour the dressing on top of the salad; toss and serve this pretty dish.

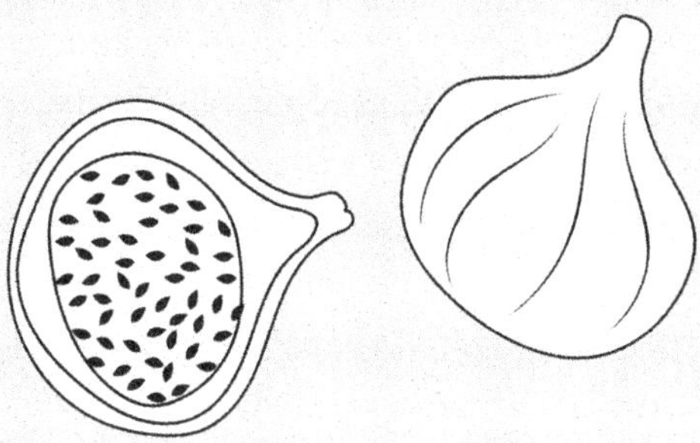

Chapter Five

Faith through Resistance, Resilience, and Justice-Making

In some church environments, persistent and uninterrupted isolation coupled with social pretense can make for stiff-necked, judgmental, and unwelcoming people. Therefore, justice movements are necessary for any vital community of faith, and have been perfecters of the faith of many a witness. I am so grateful that justice movements break out, uncontrollably, to make the church nimbler. You know, the dancer is most nimble in the heat of the dance—making moves that we don't see when the dancer is cold.

Has your congregation grown stiff-necked to essential movement work? We are charged to live the extraordinary while being present to dancing out the ordinary in daily living and social encounters. This is the very stuff of movements. Dance, children, dance! Dance out the Good News, bind up the wounds of the brokenhearted, and proclaim liberty to the captives. You know the rest of the text.

I consistently resisted the call to ministry, during an earlier career in finance as the first Black assistant vice president for a bank in my North Carolina town. Wachovia Bank and Trust, a holding company, was listed on the New York Stock Exchange and bore the distinction of not having folded during the Great Depression when all the other state banking institutions had to roll up their canopies and shutter their doors. The mountain locals bragged that "Wachovia" (a Moravian word with a silent h) was their bank because they "Watch-over-ya" money. Wachovia was the sole North Carolina bank to survive the country's worst economic downturn in history.

Wachovia Bank also had bragging rights for being a strong, progressive institution in the aftermath of being hit with a bitterly fought, racial class action suit in the 1970s, which precipitated the hiring of youngsters like me. We were called "Legacy Wachovians," because of this class action suit. We knew that our opportunities at Wachovia Bank and Trust were owed to the blessed, hell-raising youth among the employees of the late '60s and early '70s. Many of these plaintiffs in the class action lawsuit were the adult children of parents who had worked for decades on the bank's cleaning staff at night. Parents who had learned the impossible skill of becoming invisible while performing work-related tasks. Usually this meant working after business hours, when the banks were closed, so clients did not have to "experience" any racial consciousness or social awkwardness regarding race.

These parents held simple aspirations of a dayshift in the mailrooms of these large corporate entities. That would constitute career success for them, to move from the graveyard-shift janitorial staff to daytime jobs, which would allow them to see their children after school, supervise homework, attend their children's sporting events and talent shows, and enjoy dinners with their families. Simple enough? Hardly too much to ask. They were educated, respectable, law-abiding, church-going people. That was some courageous generation!

"Power concedes nothing without a struggle," as Frederick Douglass, Huey Newton, Ta-Nehisi Coates, and countless others have assured those of us who share the legacy of the lash. And we, those of my generation, did not dare squander the efforts of our forerunners by not succeeding at any opportunity presented to us. We were already schooled that we must be twice as good to get half as far. We played to win, and everybody knew it. Showing up and staying visible. Taking names!

An unseen part of being a banker, as a Black woman, is the constant activism to change public policy which impacts financial stability. During my tenure as a banker, we worked to pass the Equal Credit Opportunity Act (ECOA) to ensure women the same borrowing rights and privileges as men.

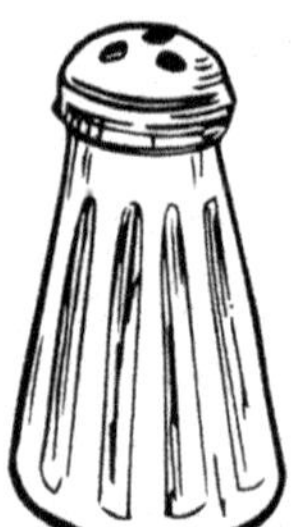

The generations of women before us could not qualify for a credit card or a home mortgage loan, no matter how stable their employment records or bill-paying habits. The ECOA made it illegal to deny a woman credit because "What if you get pregnant?" It became law that creditworthiness was the sole consideration in lending decisions for anyone. About this time, we also made great strides in the area of paid parental leave after childbirth, enforced by the US Department of Labor. Later, the Family and Medical Leave Act became law, providing employees with leave time to care for immediate family in a health crisis. Women bankers organize, agitate, and work! It is more than navy-blue suits, low-heeled pumps, and ascots.

My ten-year stint at Wachovia ended when I moved home to Atlanta to see about my diabetic mother whose health was in a state of steady decline after undergoing a below-knee amputation of her right leg. Yeah, her driving foot. She had grown more anxious and irritable each time her applications for disability were denied prior to retiring early from the Atlanta Public Schools system. My mother was a career public school teacher who graduated from Alabama's Stillman College at the age of nineteen. She completed her master's degree in early childhood education and PhD (in ABD status) at Atlanta University.

The Atlanta public schools did not participate with the US Social Security Administration; rather, it considered schoolteachers to be public babysitters. Consequently, there were no benefits for career educators. No disability benefits, even after amputation while serving in the megalopolis of the first Black high school in Georgia, Booker T. Washington High School (motto: "One Family,

One Destiny"). The school had no elevators and plenty of well-worn stone steps. We were raised near this campus with its conspicuous statue called "Booker T. Washington, Lifting the Veil of Ignorance." That statue, in front of the school, had an inscription that read, "He lifted the veil of ignorance from his people and pointed the way to progress through education and industry." But, no disability benefits, you see.

Back home in Atlanta, I was newly divorced and feverishly caring for my mother and children. I made real estate investments with my limited cash and sometimes visited the beloved historic Black church of my youth in order to placate my mother. My circle of church friends had all moved away, or died, by then.

Atlanta, at the time, belonged to the very light-skinned, processed hair, Black aristocracy. And my mother was a dark-skinned, agile, no-nonsense sister who never lost her farm-girl practicality and matter-of-fact manner. Sharp, extremely keen, righteously astute, and no stranger to hard and tedious work, she swore by the insights of Jewish educator-author Jonathan Kozol in his innovative work, *Death at an Early Age*, exposing racism within the Boston Public Schools. At nine years old, I was delighted to devote after-school hours to proofreading her dissertation. I was honored to be exposed to primary source materials on the educational disparities of our country's public-school systems. Who wouldn't see about a mother like that? I did for the last ten years of her life and would do it all over again if the circumstances were presented.

Get this, though! While stabilizing my banking career in Atlanta with a Wachovia affiliate and caring for my mother, my Wachovia Bank–employee stock doubled in value, then tripled as the North Carolina banks took over the Georgia banks in the early eighties. (God does not forget us!) That was simply a blessing that I blundered into by heeding the counsel of my superior banking officer, the tenderhearted, industrious recruiter Mr. Fred Ayers. In Georgia, as the stock split, the banks were calling these transactions "mergers," but the North Carolina banks more accurately boasted "acquisition." It was Pac-Man, baby! Perfect illustration of the banking industry in the 1980s when restrictions on interstate commerce loosened. The smaller, hometown banks were gobbled up by all the aggressive corporate giants who had strategically lobbied for these policy changes for decades. The North Carolina banks territorially consumed the Georgia banks like Pac-Man consuming digital pellets.

The larger banks were accustomed to fighting. After the Fair Housing Act was passed in 1968, banks resisted the prohibition of redlining in mortgage lending, despite heavy fines and reprimands through years of litigation. In redlining, the banks literally took a red marker and traced on a map all the Black neighborhoods that would be excluded from their mortgage loan portfolios. Right out in the open, in corporate meetings. With the support of the Federal Housing Administration. No mortgage lending to these Black folk in these urban communities. Many of the banks had branches in these same Black neighborhoods where they grew their deposit portfolios. Black people could deposit from personal earnings and robust business revenue but could not borrow from these same institutions (until the Community Reinvestment Act of 1977).

So the big banks were ready in the 1980s, with their high powered legal departments, to acquire the savings and loan institutions and to gobble up the hometown community banks. Gangsters never stopped fighting. Corporate greed was a beast that would not be tamed or contained in the banking industry!

As a commercial lender with Atlanta's First Wachovia (Wachovia's acquisition of the First National Bank of Atlanta), I unofficially "pastored" pro-athletes, dentists, attorneys, and physicians who wished to establish new practices. I counseled creative entrepreneurs and CEOs, and their children, as they planned opulent weddings, purchased their first extravagant, imported cars, and made lifetime commitments to jumbo mortgages. They came for operating capital and lines of credit, then laid bare their anxieties, their woes of exorbitant medical school debt, and their apprehensions about the lack of ethics and classism inherent in practicing law in an unjust system. They made confessions of unsavory, desperate, clandestine business tactics—some immoral, others illegal—that weighed heavily on our business consultations over brunch.

These brunches, intended to focus on the art of the deal, were always slow with something smoking and laced with some trendy drug. Raised by hard workers who knew their worth, I was adept at dealmaking, but these coffee dates frequently included more shots of Amaretto and whipped cream than actual coffee. With a maraschino cherry on top, of course! I was brought up to know that I needed all my "faculties" in this predatory world. Taking note that I refused intoxicants, my clients inevitably requested prayer for their alcoholism, addictions, and moral transgressions. Many times, we prayed about plain old broken hearts and indiscretions due to poor impulse control. Black folks in business still prayed with each other when I was a commercial lender. Working capital was not even the half of it. Atlanta's Black elite streamed in for money and desperately needed prayer—whispers of encouragement—and sound referrals for everything from lawyers to bail bondsmen to rehab centers to therapists to cheap concert tickets. I hastened to accept God's invitation to full-time ministry, eventually. I was a novice at all this well-dressed, affluent, designer pain. I was, however, familiar with the attendant issues. Because, like I say, I'm from The Bluff. You better ask somebody!

Black-eyed Peas

MUSIC *We Come a Long Way*
by Debra Snipes and The Angels

INGREDIENTS

10-ounce package mixed baby greens
1 pomegranate, peeled, seeds separated
1 small red onion, finely sliced
½ cup pecan halves (candied if you are fancy and have a sweet tooth)
1 package feta cheese
Teeny bit of Dijon mustard
Shot of red wine vinegar
Shot of extra-virgin olive oil
Lemon, room temperature for juiciness

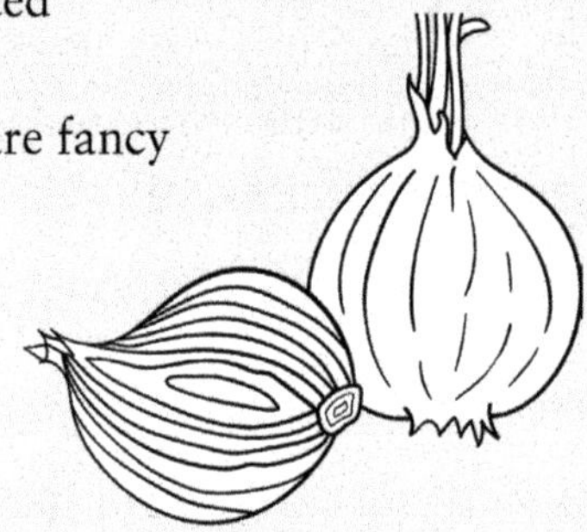

INSTRUCTIONS

This is an overnight commitment because we love them so!

Pick through and rinse peas for broken or hardened peas and stones. Let peas absorb water all night by soaking in a large bowl. Black-eyed peas are thirsty and will drink up a lot so make sure your water is a couple inches higher than the peas. After soaking, drain peas, pouring off the water.

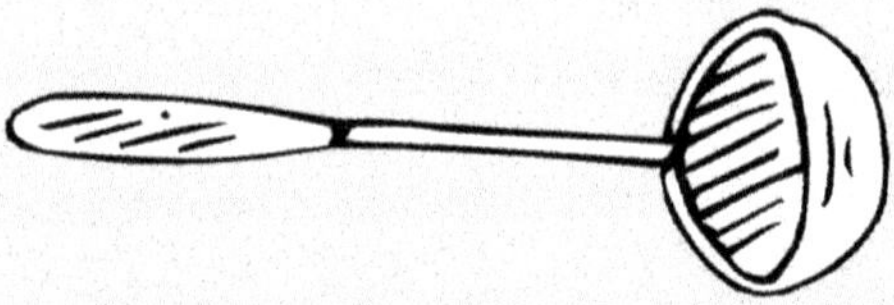

Put peas, stock, onion, celery, garlic, bay leaf, rosemary, thyme, salt, and pepper in a 6-quart slow cooker. Your crockpot, Dutch oven, or large kettle will all work fine. Put a lid on it and cook real low until tender, around 8 hours.

Take them off the heat and remove any sticks left over from herbs. You can drizzle a little olive oil on them if you'd like. Then serve, for days. Better each day!

Chapter Six

Make Us Ever More Beautiful

On my way back into life after a protracted period of full-time caring for my mother through her stroke rehabilitation, I reached out to a support group of community healthcare workers. Our home had become an auxiliary hospital, complete with all types of equipment, medications, and supplies, including a fridge of syringes and insulin for diabetes. The stroke had left my mother unable to speak coherently. Strange or cruel as it sounds, I was only able to care so intimately for my mother because she could no longer speak her "exacting" point of view to me. I really got to know her spirit when she had no command over her words, and we had a sweet relationship through this time of her recovery.

Still, it was becoming clearer that I needed to have some part of my life that was filled with beauty and joy, perhaps during my kids' school hours. My first job during my mother's recovery was working as a makeup artist for cosmetic lines created for Black women. I asked God, in prayer, if I should accept this work as a makeup artist. My big sister was a beauty expert and had taught me everything about Black skincare and glamour from an early age. And the Lord said to me, "Make people as beautiful as you can with the makeup, and I will deliver you in six weeks. Go do it with all your heart and intention." So, I did. Occasionally, my former banking clients, attorneys and physicians, would happen through Macy's, gaze at me and ask, "Is this your side hustle?"

During store hours, I took walk-ins, but for those who called for an appointment (and counseling), I made them the last customer of the day, so that as security and cleaning staff went about their duties to properly close the store, I could give the one-on-one attention that they craved. One of my first after-hours customers was a burn victim, a woman who was going on a first date to an exclusive resort in Mexico. She was self-conscious about the scarring and slight disfigurement from the burns that were completely healed.

This woman who was so scarred stepped behind the dressing screen that I used for private makeovers. She propped herself up on my bistro chair and began to cry. I could see some discoloration on her chin and decolletage, but nothing too unsightly. She asked if she could show me the scars I could not see. I said yes. After all, I was treating a bed lesion on my amputated mother's remaining ankle daily. I was using a cream called DuoDERM to accelerate skin regeneration, caring for my mother's lesion, when I learned that dark brown skin heals in small brown polka dots on a pink background of skin. The skin comes in as pink, then speckles into brown pigment. Then fully into the rich, deep-brown complexion.

Before I realized that I said yes prior to giving my client's request a thorough weighing, she had removed her blouse and undergarments to reveal substantial raised scarring that covered her torso and abdomen. I managed to look unfazed only through God's grace. She wanted to tell me what happened to cause such burns. Guided by Spirit, I put my index finger to her mouth, a universal sign that means, "hush!"

I told her with confidence, "I'm going to make all this more beautiful." The Lord had made me promise that I would make the people as beautiful as I could with the makeup. I had a special new product, used to conceal postpartum stretch marks. If I recall correctly, this concealer foundation cream was called Vantex and was in the Fashion Fair product line.

She immediately stopped crying and gazed into space with that thousand-yard stare. I took it to mean that she could not believe we could fix it up for her upcoming excursion. The stuff was waterproof, so she could even swim in it. Some part of her believed that something could be done to improve things enough for her to seek me out, make an appointment, and to show up right on time.

I worked with determination to conceal her scarring with the waterproof foundation, applying it directly, then allowing it to dry before building on another application. We were both ecstatic with the results which effectively concealed the scarring, with only a few lumps from the raised tissue on her breasts. I rejoiced with her and told her, "We got your skin covered, girl. Go get your hair and nails did!" She responded gleefully as she dressed, "The best part is that it is waterproof and does not even rub off on your clothes!" She paid for her purchase, hugged and kissed me, and left a hefty tip. I thanked God because I was that much closer to getting the bikes I had promised to my children.

"The Lord will beautify the meek with salvation" (Psalm 149:4).

It had been nearly five weeks. I was working hard with all my heart and intentionality as I heard God command. I was thinking my deliverance should be at hand because I was standing on the promises of Jesus! That very next week, my after-hours makeover appointment perched on my chair behind my elegant dressing screen. My private makeovers had evolved to the point that I had covered my dressing screens in colorful, motherland fabrics and provided cold, sparkling water for refreshment. Security had objected to the hardwood bistro chair for whatever reason . . . something about liability . . . so I replaced that chair with a barstool that had more solid steps. The stool was less comfortable for my customer, but it allowed us to do what we must. I stepped in closer to my client as she told me what she hoped to achieve in her new look. Many of my after-hours folk were looking to impress someone on a first date, sometimes an executive job interview.

I leaned in, preparing her skin with facial cleanser to give us a clean canvas for our artistry. She giggled, shyly, reminding me of when I was among the trio of the Love sisters who couldn't stop laughing through worship services despite our mamma's scowls. I caught my client's laughter and soon we both went from giggling to laughing out loud, snorting to catch our breath. I had been on my feet for thirteen hours straight, with a fifteen-minute bathroom break. I have no idea what her day held for her, but we were in the throes of the silliness of overwork and exhaustion, with fits of laughter and shaking. Neither of us dared speak the reality of how ridiculous the whole industry of makeup was for a world full of beautiful, drop-dead gorgeous human beings of God's own creation. Can't say why she was laughing but in my stupor of overwork that point was blatantly clear that all of this was quite unnecessary. It was funny.

I moved swiftly to the lower part of her face with a gentle astringent. I swept over her jaw with the damp cotton ball, leaving traces of cotton residue on her resistant skin and stubble. Confused, I tried to make sense of the amount of cotton that her jawline grabbed up as I stepped in closer applying a bit more pressure to the traces of cotton.

In her giggling fit, she closed her knees against my body regaining her balance on the barstool. I realized that my client was transgender. She muffled her embarrassed laughter upon my realization that the situation was not as I had assessed. Only for a moment, I felt a rush of fear. I was so tired, as only retail work can render a body. All that smiling, strolling around in dream-world surroundings and pretty things, on your feet eight or nine hours, on the regular. I was so delirious that I thought I may faint. As I stumbled back, not knowing what to say, she took my right hand. She spoke in calm, hushed tones:

"Honey, don't be scared. I am just here for a makeover. That's what you do, right? Everybody's talking about you and how good you make them look. Then, they feel good when they leave. Do it for me, too?" Her earnest request, sort of a plea, drew me in close like a sister. For the first time since she propped herself on my barstool, behind the dressing screen, I could see that she was gracefully beautiful. I prayed silently and asked God to guide me in making her even more radiantly gorgeous. I took my sweet time.

Every so often, she would tear up, then laugh out loud. I would fuss at her and tell her, "You better be still. And you'd better not cry and mess up my work. Hold still, let me get this waterproof eyeliner on you. Ooooo, that navy-blue eyeliner is killing on your sweet caramel skin. Girl, please don't cry."

When we were done, she hugged me so tight. I could tell she meant it. She insisted on pressing two large bills into my palm and rolling my fingers into a grasp, a gesture that means, "You must accept it."

She did look splendid! And even better, she put me back together that evening in ways that I cannot relay to someone who has never had another person coax them off the ledge, back into the sweetness of making a moment beautiful and memorable. The store was dark and closed for business with only a couple of security personnel. Security folk never minded hanging out to debrief their days because they made time and a half in overtime pay. Also, they were willing because they knew I made most of my pay after-hours with someone who could not bear their desperation in the light of day. She was my last makeover customer in that work.

I made it home from work later than usual and hugged my sleeping babies who were growing up way too fast. I checked my answering machine and heard the voice of Ira, an old banking colleague—an officer at a competing financial institution who I met when we were both new to our lending careers and Black executives were scarce. We had become instant comrades through our respective institutions. Ira's phone message was the one that made good on God's promise to deliver in six weeks.

My mother grew strong enough to go to adult daycare. My kids were within walking distance of their school. My old North Carolina banking friend arranged for me to meet with one of his high school friends who now had hiring authority at a major commercial banking institution in Atlanta. This was quite a feat, even inconceivable, because his old high school friend was a white banker. There were no white people in my Atlanta public high school. My friend and I were the same age, so I assumed his schools had been segregated as well. Not so; my friend was raised in High Point, North Carolina, right near Greensboro.

Ira was well acquainted with hard work, which was the foundation of our bond. He worked as waitstaff for most of his high school years and suffered bleeding hemorrhoids from twelve-hour shifts serving the member families of Willow Creek Country Club in High Point. The brutality of these twelve-hour country club shifts yielded an extremely polished man with country-club manners, a strategically brilliant mind, and a fierce loyalty to his friends. I count this man a blessing in my life.

His high school friend found a position within walking distance of my suburban Atlanta home. I was interviewed by a few banking officers and immediately came on as a banking center manager, just a mile from my house. My pay doubled from the compensation of my makeover gig. God had already disclosed that my offers would double my compensation. This is how I would know whether to accept the opportunity or to decline it. I could walk to work and have dinner with my kids every night. Who could ask for anything more?

I walked and worked; I set the neighborhood banking center in order, by the grace of God who makes all things possible. I faithfully turned that bank around in five weeks, implementing standard operating procedures with compassion and mutual respect. I provided internal audits and training for task clarity and risk management. This was what the friend of my dear friend said he needed. I whipped everything into shape and delivered on my commitment while raising staff morale.

One week, I got a call from a truly remarkable nonprofit CEO, who screamed into the phone, "Girl, these MacArthur folks just gave me a million dollars for the Genius Grant! I asked all around our 'Black and female' community and they tell me that you would know what to do with a million dollars. I hope you do. Do you?"

Native Southerner that I am, I responded, "Yes, ma'am!" God, as my constant companion, had prepared me for this. I gave my notice at the bank and sent thirteen individual rose bouquets to the staff of thirteen Black women at the nonprofit. My salary doubled as was promised in the spirit.

In the natural, all of this was difficult to process. I was being carried so swiftly and had to totally lean on God to move through all this. Somewhere in the glow of all of this, my mother died in my home.

I joined these women as the director of finance and human resources, basically asset management and resource management. Though I prefer organizing to management, we made great strides. In fact, we accomplished monumental deeds. I was still learning about the nonprofit international plague of infighting and skin-color microaggressions that tear at the fabric of Black women's critical work. I tolerated the hostile work environment that was wrought with class divisions until I came to understand that I would never be able to grieve in this disordered, contentious environment.

We performed beautiful, life-changing acts in healthcare advocacy. I was blessed to be central to this effort. My heart ached for the stories of misery that were ever present in our insular community. And I missed my mother so much that each morning my awakening literally startled me. How could I be alive, without her? Sometimes, I still wonder.

I did what I could while serving in this position. And what we did was pretty damn spectacular! God had shown me all that I needed to see in order to let God drive. I embarked on my journey through seminary. It was time. I was sure.

Egg Clouds

BODY BREAK

MUSIC *There Is a Balm in Gilead* by Mahalia Jackson

INGREDIENTS

4 large eggs
salt, to taste
4 teaspoons butter

INSTRUCTIONS

Whisk the eggs together with the salt until they are completely combined, and the eggs are very foamy. Melt the butter over low heat in a skillet until bubbling. Add the whisked eggs and cook, stirring constantly, until the eggs are thickened, creamy, and still shiny, about 2–3 minutes. Look for moist, even curds. Remove the scrambled eggs from the heat while they are still shiny and before they start to look dry. Serve.

Chapter Seven

Jesus Is Tenderly Calling

I have heard what I recognized to be the voice of God since I was about four years old, coming through the morning glories in our backyard. Perhaps I was hearing from God as relief from the grief of the anticipated weaning from the nursing ritual with my own mother. So many others have validated that we never stop missing our mothers. We simply adjust and limp on. I am taking their word for it.

As a grown woman, whose new friends were known as shot callers and high rollers, it was imperative to know God's voice well. I discerned what we refer to as "a call on my life." Neither the denomination of my ancestors, the National Baptist Convention, nor my neo-Pentecostal Word church supported the ordination of women as a matter of polity. "Suffer not a woman to preach, nor to usurp authority over the man, but to be in silence" (1 Timothy 2:12). Actually, this is a misquote. The scripture says "teach," not "preach." However, for our purposes, *teaching* and *preaching* are inseparable. As my preaching uncles used to say, "We got to get some learning (teaching) with our burning (preaching)!"

I believe most church women my age, or older, have heard this misquoted scripture as discouragement from preaching the gospel. As women struggling to live out the fullness of our faith—handling nearly insurmountable circumstances of working in our homes, bolstering church growth, navigating the labor market, raising children, caring for elders, covering our intimates in prayer, and conducting our various other callings and duties—no one seems overly concerned about our "suffering." But Lord have mercy, suffer not a woman to preach a Word in due season. Echo, "suffer not a woman"? This is about repression of women in ministry, pure and simple.

My seminary experience was full of glaring inequities in the resources available to women and those reserved for male seminarians. There were student apartments in seminary housing for men, while women were expected to lodge in shared dorm rooms, or in off-campus arrangements in someone's private home. Student pastoral openings and guest pulpit invitations were dedicated to male matriculators. In fact, an ecclesiastical endorsement was required for an applicant to even be considered for admission to seminary. No application was complete without the endorsement of the candidate's pastor. Hard for God to do a new thing, if the old thing must sign off on it. Harder, but not too hard for God. For with God, all things are possible. Holler, if you hear me!

The requirement for an ecclesiastical endorsement did not initially faze me, because I had served a church faithfully in time, talent, and treasure for several years. I had a congenial relationship with our "first family." In fact, our first lady and I worked out at the same studio, where I taught aerobics, a couple blocks from the church. However, when I approached my pastor, her husband, about an endorsement, at first, he expressed disappointment before becoming unable to contain his anger.

He said he wanted me to wait until our church (his new nondenominational church plant) had grown to the point that it could offer a ministerial education department. Prevaricating, he said I could get an M.Ed. degree—Ministry of Education degree, of his own design and imagination, from the school he would found and plant alongside the church. He said I could work as the school's dean to pay my children's college tuition when they were old enough to go. In an instant, he had my ministry path all figured out.

Being sure that I had heard from God concerning this—you know that blessed assurance that you get from on high—I flat-footedly told him I could not wait years because God had not indicated that I should. Courteously, I shared that God had spoken it as a more immediate matter. At that point, he could not resist telling me that I had not heard anything and that I must have had dinner too late, went to bed and thought I heard something. Needless to say, I got to stepping right on up out of that church, teen kids and all. I will not pretend that it did not break my heart to have to get another pastor to provide me with a letter of ecclesiastical endorsement after years of being open to this spiritual leader and giving faithful service at my own church. However, God meant it for my good (Romans 8:28).

God says, "See if I will not open you the windows of heaven, and pour you out a blessing, that there shall not be room enough to receive it" (Malachi 3:10); and so, I did exactly that. I never missed an opportunity to prosper by sowing a financial seed into the ministry that fed me spiritually for many years, always expecting a hundredfold return. From my "prosperity" pastor at the neo-Pentecostal church where I raised my children, I learned that God's word "shall not return unto me void, but it shall accomplish that which I please, and it shall prosper in the thing whereto I sent it" (Isaiah 55:11). God never does anything vain, void, or unproductive.

You can depend on Jesus, box and straight!

This neo-Pentecostal pastor unflinchingly taught that prosperity through tithing is a spiritual law. That if we abide in that law, we will see the return, not only in our finances but in other matters that we think are too much for us to abide. Our health, our relationships, the pursuit of justice. He taught us line upon line, precept upon precept—even if he was a notoriously narcissistic, controlling leader. Just this year, this same pastor recanted all his teachings about tithing, explaining that he was mistaken. He said he was preaching an Old Testament doctrine while pastoring a New Testament church. This, after he had become a multimillionaire from his misinterpretation of scripture. I have got to reiterate that God made good on our pastor's misunderstanding and honored our willingness to tithe. The Word does not return void, even when human beings are confused. God chooses and God uses. Use me too, please, Jesus!

My grandfather and uncles were Baptist pastors, so my confidence was not shaken by all the angry, disrespectful men working in ministry or aspiring to ministry. I did wonder how I would ever be able to work collaboratively with any of them while maintaining my ethics, self-respect, and human dignity. However, in the words of the song popularized by the Reverend Timothy Wright, "God's got a way that you can't go under; you must come in at the door." After graduating from Cornell with honors and fulfilling my community service with a decade of a commercial banking career, my ministerial call became unrelenting and I firmly decided to advance my studies at our local Black seminary.

The Interdenominational Theological Center (ITC), Atlanta's urban Black seminary nestled among renowned Historically Black Colleges and Universities and magnolia trees, was only blocks from The Bluff, the tough, cohesive neighborhood of my youth. Though my life-long yearning to recover my full self while healing the world has flung my "soul-home" far and wide, my first cousins still worship at their church in The Bluff.

In seminary, I loved the way my professors "preached" their lectures, complete with joyful sermonic celebration as the classes closed. During the last ten to fifteen minutes of class, all the MDiv candidates were on our feet, arms waving, weeping and preaching back, testifying to the goodness of God. That was my greatest joy in seminary!

I was enraptured by our preaching professors: Black, strong, sober, and clearheaded. I ran to each of my classes to unravel any societal concerns with their sonorous and energetic homiletics and delivery. Preach to me, brothers! Oh, yes!

I loved Dr. Kenneth Henry's church history class and could not resist bringing guests with me so I could debrief afterward. So great was my joy at these sermonic celebrations that I insisted my otherwise reserved and scholarly son, Alan, who would go on to graduate college at nineteen years old, come to see this beautiful example of Black manhood. Alan went to class with me and was filled by this experience, as well. Or at least he said so. Glory be to God!

Still, I met with the usual resistance to women in ministry and downright hostility to any Black woman seeking ordination in the historic Black church in the Bible Belt. I was often made aware that I was not who was wanted or anticipated. Resentment and bitterness permeated the air of this institution of ministerial preparation. The frequent agony and the rare joys were so intense, at times, that I wondered if I could make it through.

The preachers in my family instilled an adoration of the preached Word because it spoke to our struggles as oppressed people. The contentment felt when I heard the Word preached enabled me to take on my life and support the community through tireless service, in the power of God's might. Yet the community of believers was still immersed in the doctrine, spoken and unspoken, that women are not to be accepted into ordained ministry. The brothers had "something" that they were not about to share: our historic Black churches. These were the places where they held CEO positions and owned corporate real estate. Not so in the wider society. Thus, they defended their possession and power, ferociously!

As a woman who takes myself appropriately seriously, I was depressed by the phenomena of sisters being the "engine" of the church but excluded from all significant ministry pursuits. I did not know any women who were pastors, but I knew too many women who participated in the church's hostilities. There was the time I showed up in

West African–influenced attire and a regal Gele headwrap—the trademarks of my neighborhood and the influence of the Nation of Islam which taught us entrepreneurship, self-respect, and self-love. My professor, a renowned ethnomusicologist, adamantly clapped her hands loudly, while remarking, "Why is it that the yellow-est nigger in the class always shows up in African clothes?"

I could feel my heart throbbing in my ears. My eyes burned. That was some of the hurt I mentioned earlier about colorism. In retrospect, I know that ten years of caregiving for my mother left me poorly equipped for the aggressive behavior of those who only worked in my neighborhood during the day but lived in Atlanta's sprawling suburban homes inhabited by the Black aristocracy. The seminary was in my neighborhood, The Bluff. We were kind in neighborly relations, humble, gracious, and soft-spoken people. This heartless woman only came to the neighborhood to ensure her paycheck and scurried out prior to sunset. We were nothing to her.

I must have been looking powerfully good that day to evoke such a strong reaction from this miserable old woman. I have gained this wisdom as an older woman myself: Not everybody is going to be kind or respectful of you. Sometimes, people are threatened.

Cut to the core by the callousness of this highly influential professor, I lost myself in prayer for several days. Praying and cogitating. Spirit eventually spoke to me from Isaiah 50:7, "For the Lord God will help me; therefore shall I not be confounded: therefore have I set my face like a flint, and I know that I shall not be ashamed." I journeyed on with a face of flint and this personalized spiritual revelation, straight from the Source. I grew in boldness, focus, and determination. My first year after completing seminary, I met the Reverend Dorri Sherrill who was an ordained woman in the United Church of Christ. She was eager to share with me the possibilities for women to be ordained in the UCC. Because Dorri is a white woman, I took her testimony with a grain of salt, knowing from years of enduring structural racism that what may be open to her as a white woman may not be open to me. But we kept talking for months, until I could hear her.

Rev. Dorri would become the personification of "life, more abundantly" on my ministerial path. I was reminded, once more, that I am enough, fully competent, and even sweeter than deserved. The psalmist writes, "I will praise thee; for I am fearfully and wonderfully made: marvelous are thy works; and that my soul knoweth right well" (Psalm 139:14). Knoweth right well, y'all! You heard?

Baked Salmon

MUSIC *Softly and Tenderly Jesus is Calling* by Will Lamartine Thompson

INGREDIENTS

2 pounds whole salmon, skin-on preferred
2 tablespoons butter, melted or olive oil
2 cloves garlic, minced
1 tablespoon brown sugar
1 teaspoon Italian seasoning
1 teaspoon ground paprika
1 teaspoon garlic powder
¾ teaspoon salt

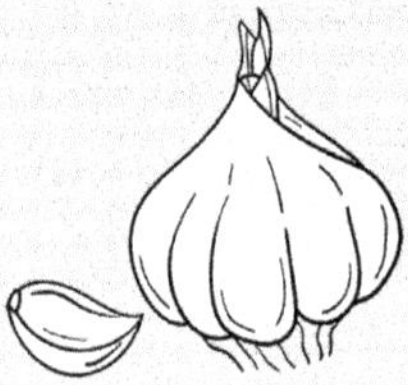

INSTRUCTIONS

Preheat the oven to 375 degrees F. Line a rimmed baking sheet with foil. Place the salmon, skin side down, pink side up, on the prepared baking sheet.

Crimp the edges of the foil around the salmon to make what appears like a boat to catch the juices when baking.

In a small bowl, combine the melted butter and the minced garlic. Brush half of the garlic butter over the salmon.

In another small bowl, combine the brown sugar, Italian seasoning, paprika, garlic powder, and salt. Evenly sprinkle the spice mixture over the salmon. Drizzle the coated salmon with the remaining garlic butter.

Bake the coated salmon until it reaches your preferred doneness, between 125–145 degrees F, about 15–22 minutes. If desired, carefully baste the salmon with the juices halfway through baking.

Allow the cooked salmon to rest for 5 minutes after baking. Serve.

Chapter Eight

Working 'til Jesus Comes

By the time of my first call to pastor a church in North Carolina, I was so numb from microaggressions of gender bias, racism, classism, colorism, and internalized racism, that I hardly noticed the combative and unkind behaviors of some church members and lay leaders of my new parish. Problem is, detachment is never effective protection from the impact on the autonomic nervous system when racism is acted out interpersonally, supported institutionally, and enlivened systemically. I suffered from anxiety and did not consciously understand why.

I made it through my initial pastoral appointment with lots of prayer and supplication, then moved on to Seattle to launch an educational ministry on the appropriate clergy response to intimate partner violence. Midlife paranoia and "pageant-like" competition among the select ensemble of clergywomen there made this educational-ministry setting a place of histrionics and egomania. Still, it was a very special landing place founded by the inimitable Rev. Dr. Marie Fortune—God bless her courageous soul!—and I made a couple of lifelong friends there.

There was much to experience and create in the Pacific Northwest by organizing and training communities of clergy in this call for a couple of years. Lots of travel and talking-head appearances before large audiences. I preached everywhere, wrote tons of curricula, and lived in airports. I basked in the beautiful Orcas Island of the San Juan Islands, in Washington state. I flourished in the eighteen hours of daylight that produced fuchsia floral palettes that I had never seen in nature. I skipped through Skagit Valley Tulip Festivals with my best friend Robert, a national of Thailand, a gay man who was almost as tender as my mother in his attention and care. He vowed to teach me the transit system in Seattle as if I were "new to the States." Always with deep compassion for anyone relocating to Seattle from the Deep South, Robert generously offered what he called "immigrant lessons." God knows, with no car and most of my personal effects stolen as I traveled, I desperately needed those lessons. He brought me corn bread from the bakery and made his favorite chrysanthemum tea. My brother, my friend, Robert.

My closest women friends were Deah, an aerial artist from Louisiana who moved to United Arab Emirates to teach ESL, and Masooma, a proud Muslimah who understood so well how to sister, as Muslimahs do. Masooma could keep a confidence, empathize, and pump up a deflated spirit. Lord, I wanted to stay with each of them, forever. But I needed the people who walked, everyday and all day, with the horrific history of our country's violently enforced separation and segregation. I needed East Coast people who were grounded in the human predicament.

Except for Jay, my Native American comrade—a Lakota man who bore a striking resemblance to the young Elvis—I felt these friends could not fully hold the legacy of chattel slavery or even comprehend its enduring negative impact on efforts to give and receive love. Though we could not step through each other's looking glass, we loved hard, regardless. A beautiful circle. No regrets.

But I longed for the clearly defined human rights understandings of the South, its stark examples of violations and what not to do to other human beings. Southerners have been in this "isms" conversation a long time. Historically, Southern white people would just as soon give up their citizenship before accepting that Black people are fully human and endowed by the Creator with certain inalienable rights. I am referring to the Civil War, which some of my liberal, Southern, white co-laborers—activists and people who work for social change—still call "the War of Northern Aggression." In the South, everything about race and class is right out there in the open. We can agree that there is an elephant in the room. Our language is direct and the sentiments overt, even if the communication is occasionally "nice/nasty."

I was missing that level of honesty in conversation and relationships. It is difficult to trust people who perpetuate the sophisticated methodology of racism by their nuance and enactment of restrictive zoning laws, polite ordinances, and implied exclusions. I was homesick for the South. Exhausted by ministry hobnobbing and banquet food on the road, and the characteristic infighting of egotistical players and doggedly determined careerists, I was rapidly becoming superficial in my own deepest passions. The games people play can make you bitter, but for unceasing prayer. Bitterness is the guest who eats up its host, I've heard it said in "the rooms." Twelve-step rooms. I have treated issues with excess food when I could not remember God would handle the matters that I cannot.

I moved back home to Atlanta, this time to nurture my soul's desire and to launch an organization devoted to cultivating a culturally appropriate, faith-based response to intimate partner violence. The Black Church and Domestic Violence Institute was launched to continue my work in this educational ministry. Black churches are plentiful in Atlanta. For that matter, there is no shortage of domestic violence in Atlanta, either. In collaboration with mainline denominations and judicatories, The Black Church and Domestic Violence Institute serves clients such as the US Department of Health and Human Services, the US Department of Justice, the Centers for Disease Control and Prevention, and the National Coalition Against Domestic Violence.

As I worked this specialized ministry with the support and loyalty of a remarkable staff, my already extensive travel increased. Speaking and training invitations, including the President's clergy breakfast forums, and the demand of federally sponsored consultations, compelled me to forge a stronger connection with the Appalachian church of my first pastoral call. I was moving fast and striving for balance. I needed a church! I was gentle enough with myself to add in the practice of sabbath rest for a day or two between trips. With my kids in college by now, I needed a simple church home where the people knew me in all my glory, agony, and rage. I longed for a place to serve often through preaching, liturgical dance, trustee work, and a lectionary lunchtime discussion group. A place to be vulnerable and to receive the corporate love of the Body of Christ. I heard the Lord say my healing could be found, there, at that church in the Blue Ridge.

I already knew these folk, the good, the bad, and the detestable. What's more is that they already knew me. We had collectively worked hard on our relationships. Without this parish ministry service at First Congregational UCC of Asheville, I would not have been as effective in the ministry to appropriately address violence against women, and clergy ethics training. I worshipped and served there for the next fifteen years. The discipline of regular service keeps us sane, you know. Give, and it shall be given unto you. I will say it again, service keeps us sane. Worth repeating. Damn near a mantra!

Southern Collard Greens

BODY BREAK

with Garlic and Olive Oil

MUSIC *We'll Work Till Jesus Comes* by Elizabeth King Mills

INGREDIENTS

1 to 2 bunches of collard greens
1 large garlic clove
olive oil

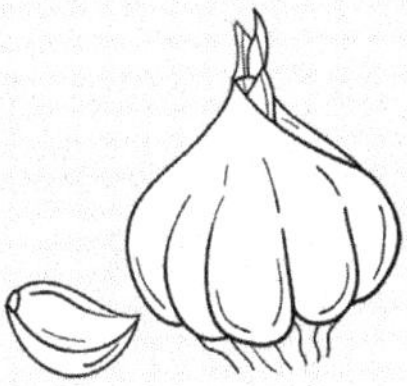

INSTRUCTIONS

Grab a large stock pot.

Get a bunch of collards. If you live in one of those geographic areas, like the Northeast or Mid-Atlantic states, where they think 6–8 leaves are a bunch, you need to get at least a couple bunches. Cut off the root ball close to the leaves, like you would with thirsty cut wildflowers. Then, put them in water in ample vase, Kool-Aid pitcher or a wide-mouth jar for a day so they can plump up to their fullest. Don't refrigerate collards while they are in the vase hydrating. Reminds me (and you) that a kitchen is a wholesome, healthy greenspace when I have these arrangements on the counter, drinking up water.

The next day, or several hours later, when you are satisfied that they are plumped up, take the leaf by the stump of the stem, and cut the heavy stem away from the leaf. We want mostly leaf. Stems can be composted or fed to the chickens if they happen to reside with you. Stack several leaves together, roll 'em up! Cut them no more than an inch wide.

Finely chop up a large garlic clove to add a generous amount of garlic love!

After pouring enough olive oil to cover the bottom of the pot, set on low heat and toss in your garlic, first. Very briefly, enjoy the aroma, then add cut collards, stirring slowly to blend flavor. Don't linger and let that garlic burn before adding the collards.

When the greens look cooked (around 5 minutes of gentle stirring), add a teeny bit of water, cut off burner and cook in residual heat for 15 more minutes. Yum!

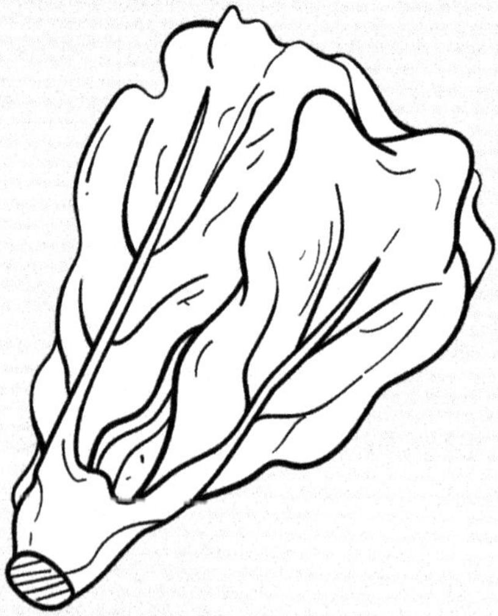

Chapter Nine

Pain, the Great Teacher

Any proponent of aware embodiment, as I am, must offer a discourse on pain, whether spiritual or physical. When we are fully in our bodies, we know that there is no separation. Working-class persons, particularly laborers, receive this enlightenment very early in their lives. I learned early that Jesus is the embodiment of God. "God is near to the brokenhearted and delivers those who are crushed in spirit" (Psalm 34:18).

I have pushed my body and mind way beyond their intended limits often to satisfy the needs, desires, and demands of a seemingly insatiable owning-class society. There is a persistent subjugation in living Black and female in a nation that freely dispenses violent repression to maintain the interests of the dominant class.

This sacrifice of the body and spirit for approval, viability, and survival becomes habitual and compulsive. We are divinely designed to receive messages of pain to train us and redirect us into health and wellness. When we overextend, pain calls us back to our finiteness. No doubt, pain is our most effective teacher!

My faith tradition during my formative years held to the belief of spiritual healing by prayer and the laying on of hands. As the often-quoted expression goes, "Just a touch from Jesus will make everything all right." This was not entirely untrue in my case; I have experienced deliverance from all manner of infirmities through the power of divine touch in the laying on of hands.

Yet, there was a point where I was in so much pain that I simply had to acknowledge the clear testimony of my autonomic nervous system, with special attention on my parasympathetic nervous system—the part which orders rest and proper digestion for the body.

Making it plain, I could not eat or sleep in this global society that is perpetually hostile to any sentient being who is Black and female. I had been "slain in the Spirit" during the Baptism of the Holy Ghost. I was empowered with my heavenly language (glossolalia), speaking in tongues. However, my body still ached from the emotional stress of work and unsupported parenting, excess weight, and the residual adrenaline, all caused by negotiating the terms of my life and the lives of those who counted on me.

I relied on my sporadic yoga practice. Sporadic, because deep inside I still believed that only the faith healings of my ancestors could relieve my pain and heal the brokenness that was a direct result of experiencing a constant flow of indignities and predatory actions in the essential transactions of daily life.

I'd gone to doctors to try to resolve this pain I was experiencing, to no avail. While founding and leading a successful national nonprofit to train clergy and other practitioners in an appropriate response to intimate partner violence, I began to notice the agonizing pain of witnessing account after horrendous account of violence and repression. The added responsibilities of fund development, meeting payroll, honoring commercial leases, maintaining a national board, and enduring basic misogynoir run wild, contributed to the need for me to slow down, let go, and BE.

Through a somatic therapist, I learned how to talk about the pain in terms that went beyond simply, “Ouch!” There was an in-depth study, teaching cumulative experiences and precise language that I learned by referencing *Waking the Tiger* by Peter A. Levine. I learned that the way I received hostile energy was stored in my body. It took much guidance and time to understand how to allow this unwanted energy to flow through my body. I learned it well and consider this flow to be an integral part of my daily yoga practice and meditation.

During this phase of body/mind/spirit discernment, I engaged in a diligent search for experienced guides. My life was shrinking in the desperation of the pain that refused to respond to medication, naturopathic treatment, prayer, physical therapy, or somatic experiencing. With prayer and a measure of urgency, I was led to Nirgunavathi and Sri Ekan and learned that committing to my yoga practice—devoting myself to the teachings and “love languaging” of a compassionate yogini and sri—would make a difference. I shared the hopelessness of my pain with Nirgunavathi and Sri Ekan; I shared that the overwhelming pain was dictating the limits of my relationships and vision. After two or three sessions, I moved to Winter Park, Florida, for the community of Lake Center Yoga in Longwood, Florida.

The pain was so ever-present that I did not even consider how I would manage financially. Pain makes life very simple.

This hurts. That does not. I thank God that I had the good sense to move toward that which does not hurt.

I was beginning to release the pain that had accompanied me for years, leading me to somatic experiencing—a process that allows the body to gently drop into an earlier experience of trauma and/or stress and release the negative energies through a series of exercises such as body scanning, aware breathing, postures, and asanas. Sri and Nirgunavathi told me of a fellow traveler, Skip, who was strategizing his own recovery from persistent pain through the practice of yoga, the study of the Bhagavad Gita, lifegiving nutrition, and participating in Satsang to uplift his spirit and deepen community connections. This fellow traveler was interested in sharing his home, as his previous housemate was a pilot who had recently relocated to accommodate a preferred flying route. There was little in my life that would make me comfortable staying in the home of a man whom I did not know, let alone a southern, white man. But that is just how deep the pain was—it was stronger, more urgent than my fear.

Skip became my example in the journey to release pain. My mornings became prayers and sun salutations. I had previously relied on a somatic therapist who taught me how to discontinue the holding of pain in my body. I learned from her to allow the energy of the pain to pass through my body into the earth below, which could contain infinite amounts of it. I began to love the earth even passionately as it received all of my pain without having to confer with me about next steps or an appropriate disposition of that unwanted energy. The earth simply received and affirmed me with, "I can handle the pain you are holding. Give it to me. You are more grounded, now."

While sharing Skip's house, I noticed his mornings were often filled with headstand and handstand inversions, meditation, and prayer. He and his Jack Russell terrier, Clifford, were Episcopalians with pain that was comparable to mine, if the dog's cry was any indication.

These four—Sri and Nirgunavathi, Skip and Clifford—transformed my relationship to pain and my sense of placement within community. This home of compassion and encouragement settled me enough to experience my placement on the North American continent as the great-granddaughter of Mary Myers, formerly enslaved; granddaughter of Gassenie Hobson, school principal, farmer, and mother of twelve; daughter of Annie Mary Webb, public school teacher and elder sister of a tribe of educators, farmers, and pastors. Then, there's me! Aubra Love, yet unfolding and born again, again, and again with a love too vast to be possessed or contained; mother, giving sweet birth to Tahira Love Brooks, a world traveler, brilliant homeschooling mom, code-cracking IT specialist, writer, and spoken-word artist, who blessed us with Dylan Wendy Goldson, a prayer and a promise manifested by the hand of our lactating God.

Avocado Tomato Salad

BODY BREAK

MUSIC *We Belong to the Earth* by Magpie

INGREDIENTS

¼ cup extra-virgin olive oil
Juice of 1 lemon
¼ teaspoon ground cumin
Kosher salt
Freshly ground black pepper
3 avocados, cubed
1 pint cherry tomatoes, halved
1 small cucumber, sliced into half moons
⅓ cup corn
1 jalapeño, minced (optional)
2 tablespoons freshly chopped cilantro

INSTRUCTIONS

In a small bowl, whisk together oil, lemon juice, and cumin. Season dressing with salt and pepper.

In a large serving bowl, combine avocados, tomatoes, cucumber, corn, jalapeño, and cilantro.

Gently toss with dressing and serve immediately.

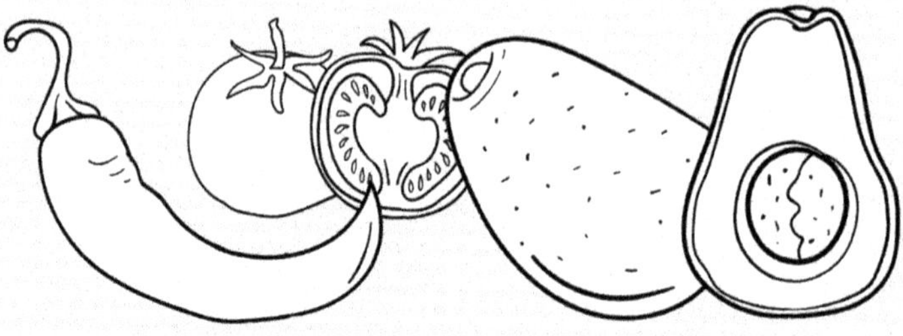

Chapter Ten

Quick Transitions

I was way out in the woods at the campsite of the Episcopal Diocese of Western North Carolina, at Lake Logan. I had become enraptured by this site during an earlier visit when I was invited as a guest preacher by William Mance of St. Matthias' Episcopal Church. Bill and Diane Mance, a gracious Asheville couple, were so warm and welcoming that I wanted our whole church to enjoy the site by holding our annual church retreat there. Our church retreat planners were enthusiastic about the idea, and Lake Logan became "our place" for off-the-grid fellowship.

One summer, while we were out in the sticks, I was scheduled to preach on Sunday morning at our church retreat. I suffered an aortic aneurysm on that Saturday night. My aorta just fell away from my heart. My church membership of doctors, midwives, doulas, private-duty nurses, and massage therapists—people who do not fear the body—kept me alive until an ambulance arrived from a neighboring town. The children of the church, whom I knew very well, had puzzled looks on their little faces as they massaged my feet and legs while I lay atop a craft table, sweating profusely and unable to breathe.

In these circumstances, we just hand over our bodies to medical teams and hope for the best, usually having little to no control over whether the proper reverence will be shown. I just grabbed a heartful of those "trusts" scriptures and went on through the inevitable surgery. "Though he slay me, yet will I trust him." By the time my gurney was wheeled into the emergency operating room, inclusive language was no longer of interest to me, as my King James upbringing rapidly kicked in and effectively ministered to me from Job 13:15 and other Elizabethan-English verses.

I woke up from a death-defying heart surgery with no voice, surgical wounds, "freeze plugs" draining from my rib cage, nerve damage, and a paralyzed vocal cord, unable to speak or swallow. A contraption was breathing for me and monitoring my blood pressure by squeezing and squishing my left bicep, with a loud hum accompanying each squeeze.

My aorta was the primary issue, but the recurrent laryngeal nerve that lives right next to my aorta was also damaged, rendering me unable to speak a word for three full years. I suspect the injury occurred in the slip of a lifesaving surgical instrument on soft tissue, damaging the large nerve that controls my vocal cords, breathing, and swallowing. Could have been a careless intubation. Can't say for sure. But I could not make a sound, not even an om for meditation. Before this I had a "Bernice Johnson Reagon, Sweet Honey in the Rock" voice. No isht!

My cardiologist, Dr. Marc Groh, who I met in the emergency room, visited me after my surgery when I was between this world and the next. He had come by many times before in the wee hours. I was aware of his presence but could not indicate any awareness to him no matter how much I willed it.

One day, he said, "I am the one who performed your surgery." Poking my left collarbone, he said, "You have everything you need in there, now. Are you coming back?"

I heard him and responded, "Where is everybody?" I wanted the presence of my children because I knew that I was their strongest advocate in an often-unwelcoming world.

Dr. Groh, a little startled that I was speaking, advised me that my voice was but a whisper. I could not yet tell because I was so loud "inside." He went on to tell me that, as a voice professional, I should begin my application for disability because it is a slow process, frequently six months to a year. My son sprang into action to make sure that all paperwork, interviews, and processing happened in a timely manner.

Several days later, while still in the hospital, a sturdy attendant came to help me out of bed while humming "In the Garden." When we were in the corridor passing the nurses' station, he began singing in a bellowing voice. I held onto him, and we wept together. The doctors and nurses stopped to applaud—his beautiful singing, I thought, which filled my parched soul. But with dropped jaws and eyes wide, they declared it a miracle that I was alive and walking, leaning on the attendant's arm.

The doctors and several of the nurses were members of my own church in the Blue Ridge, where relationships had begun with such tension, strain, and mean-spiritedness. I know they were involved in the sacred work that brought me back to my family. With the satisfaction that I was yet alive to gaze upon the faces of my sweet babies, again, the rest of our foul history at that church did not even matter!

Those babies of mine can make me forget about every unpleasant thing that ever happened. They make everything alright. Even as solid adults, who love so generously, they have that effect on me. All is right with everything when they are present!

From the Blue Ridge Mountains I moved to my daughter and son-in-law's home in Maryland for recovery. My daughter, Tahira, cared for me physically after the heart surgery that silenced me for three years, with respiratory issues, paralyzed vocal cords, and wound-care issues. I had begun working with a speech therapist at Johns Hopkins Voice Care Center following a second surgery to deal with my paralyzed vocal cord. Amused by my intact, unapologetic Southern accent, the speech therapist was stifling laughter during each of our sessions. I didn't like that at all, but there were more critical issues to take care of—like a plumbing issue in North Carolina—so I gave her a pass and got on with my life.

The trip back to North Carolina was expected to be brief. I had been assured by my friend who has cared for my family for decades in so many ways, including this property I owned, that he had the situation well in hand. Then, I received the disturbing news of his emergency admittance to the hospital with a bacterial infection that left him so ill he was barely conscious. Heavy with guilt that this may be due to the work he performed for me, and knowing that negotiating with medical professionals has always been difficult for him because highly nuanced English is not his first language, I threw a bag in the car and drove on down to North Carolina, with a quickness. To advocate for him, to show some respect, and to take care of my business.

Lemon Butter Salmon

BODY BREAK

MUSIC *Spirit, Spirit of Gentleness* by James K. Manley

INGREDIENTS

4–6 ounces of skinless salmon
2 teaspoons Old Bay seasoning
2 tablespoons olive oil
¼ cup chicken broth
Squeeze of lemon juice
2 tablespoons honey
Fresh parsley
Lemon slices for presentation

INSTRUCTIONS

Make sure salmon is room temperature for about 15 minutes. During that time, prepare the lemon butter sauce by melting a teaspoon of butter over medium heat. Add chicken broth and lemon juice. Simmer sauce, about 3 minutes. Stir in butter and honey, then set aside. Pat both sides of salmon with a paper towel, season with Old Bay.

In a non-stick skillet, heat olive oil over medium-high heat. Cook salmon in olive oil to your taste. Serve with a drizzle of lemon butter sauce, garnish with lemon slices and parsley, for presentation.

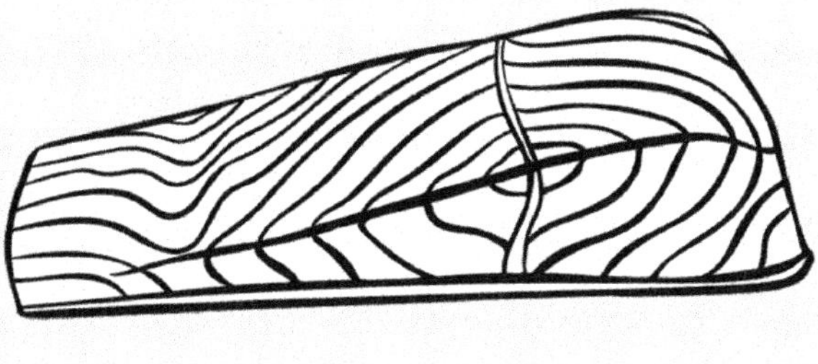

Chapter Eleven

A Plumber, a Prayer, a Pal

I knew that I was back home in the Blue Ridge Mountains the moment I entered the Ingles chain grocery store in Western North Carolina and could smell only fried chicken and peach cobbler—a stark contrast from entering the Whole Foods store near where I was living in Maryland. Whole Foods in downtown Silver Spring is cooking all day, but you can smell nothing food-related. Smells more like patchouli to ease stress and anxiety, I guess.

In the Blue Ridge Mountains food market, I could hear Tina Turner's raspy singing thumping from the best Bose speakers, as middle-aged, white women mouthed the lyrics to "What's Love Got to Do with It?" while reading packages and cans for content. I noticed that the white women were not dressed in black business suits and pumps, or even that mountain-woman hiking gear, but they were in high heels and animal print. No L.L.Bean for this group, just finely tailored sweaters, silk blouses, and pencil skirts, with jewelry and accent neck scarves. They had tastefully applied makeup, hairdos, and warm, open-faced smiles. They looked different from the white women where I live now. Friendly, more relaxed. Not all rigid and uptight. Good Lord, I'm home!

Making good time on my errands, I pulled up to check on the job of my plumber who was hoping to remedy a clogged main sewer line. The repair had been intermittently troublesome since Thanksgiving. One of the plumbers had answered my call to clear the drain line when I was informed that the pipe cleanout on the yard was throwing up fecal refuse. It had happened before. Not too alarming. However, the plumber who responded could not retrieve his cable from the drainpipe. The owner of the plumbing company came out to assess the situation, promptly cut the cable, and then sent his worker on to the next job with other equipment, I suppose. That took care of his issue but didn't do much for mine.

As I approached a young laborer on the yard in the freezing-cold weather, he said almost too cheerfully, "You come to take a gander?" I repeated in my head, "A gander? This country child! Good Lord, I'm home!"

I said, "Yes, young man, tell me about what you've done." With that clear-eyed, sincere, innocent country look, he apologetically responded, "If I'da known you was comin', I wouldn't-a covered up this part. But, come on, let me show you." He meticulously explained each part of his work, proudly displaying the newly installed two-way cleanout and freshly laid PVC. He went on to explain that I could now go either way when I needed to access the cleanout for any future clogs.

I took pictures of the work with my phone and hurried back to my car to retreat from the cold. He followed me up the hill to open my car door, because how else would I get in my car? I managed to control my panic that I was being followed by a man with a heavy tool in his hand. Once I was seated in the warmth of my car, he asked if he might ask me for a favor. Because I had been away from this "neighborly" Appalachian culture for a while, and it was unmercifully cold outside, I silently stared ahead hoping it was not going to be something I did not want to do. "Could you maybe pray for my friend who got caught up in drugs around Christmastime and we ain't heard tell of him since? We do not know what happened to him. He's like a brother to me. He'd be right here on this job with me if we knew where he was at. I know you're a preacher. My boss-man told me. Pray for my friend?"

I got out of the car, took both his large, calloused hands in mine and began to cover his friend, him, his mamma, and daddy in prayer for blessings in the new year. "Lord Jesus, we thank you that we can call on your holy name anytime, anyplace, 24/7/365, because that's just the kind of Savior you are! Aw, we are so grateful that we have the good sense to bring it to you because sometimes it is too, too much for us. Now, Lord as we begin this year, I am down here talking to you on behalf of my brother and his struggling friend. Lord Jesus, you know him and his friend better than I could ever know them, but what you've shown me is that you are a good and loving Savior who will see about any of your children who petition you in earnest with a heart of thanksgiving. We are grateful, right now, because your promises are true. Your promises are *yes* and *amen*. Wherever this friend is, Lord, please protect him from any hurt, harm, or danger. We know you see him clearly as we wonder of his whereabouts. Won't you wrap your loving arms around him and give him a heart to return home to his friends, family, and loved ones. And please Jesus, strengthen the young man whose hands I hold. And when I release him, I am placing his hands in your Almighty hands, knowing that you are faithful and just. That you are a burden bearer. That you said, 'Come unto me, all ye who labor and are heavy laden and I will give you rest.' We can count on you, Jesus. We call it done, in your mighty name. And we'll be so careful to give your name all the glory and all the praise. In your matchless, and mighty sweet and precious name, Jesus! *Aaaamen.*"

It was so cold that we were panting and tearing, as our breath vaporized like rings of smoke during my praying and his intermittent "Thank you, Jesus" repetitions. I looked into his steely, blue eyes as he opened the car door for me, a second time. "You done a good thing, thank you," was all he said before hastening back to finish his work before dark.

I grabbed the hand sanitizer from under my car seat, as if to leave the moment and circumstances with him and Jesus. I have been known to carry things I need to let go of, if there is no ritual of release. Hand sanitizer worked fine for me that day as a ritual of release. Have thine own way, Lord. You are the potter. I am the clay!

I headed back to Ingles, the fried chicken and peach cobbler supermarket chain, to pick up "the trinity" as my chef friend, a US Air Force veteran, calls it. The trinity? That is the celery, onions, and carrots; "mirepoix," she also calls it. Couple of potatoes, and I am ready to get the crockpot going so I am not tempted to spend hundreds of dollars on eating out.

I checked in with the master plumber to ask when the worker on my job would be done, and left a message saying that I would stay in town until the job was complete. He had told me earlier that he did not feel right about charging me for work that was all underground unless I got to see it for myself. Having known the master plumber for years, I trusted him enough to not have to drive eight hours in below-freezing temps for this repair. Nevertheless, this is the Appalachian way of cutting a fair deal. I must honor and respect that. Thank you, God, for this honest mountain man who puts people before profit.

I was off to my broker's office to discuss possibilities of how I could better manage these absentee-owner property issues. Jo, my broker, and I met over a healthy lunch to go over everything. Jo is a Brit, very funny and energetic with flowing cascades of perfumed red tresses. We bantered through our indecision about where to go for lunch. I was not sure how much time she could allot. She had just lost a major tenant, a law firm, in the corporate complex that she owns downtown. She was not sure what restaurant I could afford, given the plumbing situation and all my health setbacks. And this luncheon was definitely on me this time.

This is okay with me because Jo's favorite restaurant is Chick-fil-A. And you know what? I made the first corporate loan to Chick-fil-A while a Wachovia Bank loan officer at Atlanta's Greenbriar Mall office. Chick-fil-A's founder, Truett Cathy, was a Christian man who did business with so much loving-kindness that I felt as if I had been to church whenever he left my office. They still do not open for business on Sunday. I was saddened by the clash in ideologies as the Cathy family waded through its controversies resulting from their closed-mindedness and oppositional actions to the lived realities of Christians who are LGBTQIA2S+.

Jo and I chose the women-owned East Village Grille, instead of Chick-fil-A, mostly for their wonderfully diverse menu and the strong female presence in the ambience. We both know, all too well, the experience of married couples and men being seated and served before solo women diners. Food is good at the East Village Grille, and the service is respectful and friendly to unescorted women.

Jo had to tell me about all her romantic escapades since we last spoke. There was quite a bit to share. But before too terribly long she yielded and offered me a chance to share. She is empathetic enough to know that I may want to say something. This pause for me to "spill the tea" about my romantic involvements is usually uncomfortably silent. I am quiet by nature and single by choice. My mamma would kid me and my then-husband Rutherford, saying, "I don't know how my grandbabies ever learned to talk. Y'all just hang around each other, grinning all day!"

Romance is not where my focus is during a business luncheon. I treasure Jo's company, but we are not actual girlfriends. So, I told her that romance is generally not where my head is, while doing business. Granted, I have had some deeply romantic phases in my life, some involving years of commitment, marriage, joint finances, children, and mutual plans. However, it has been a long time and I now have other priorities, by choice and necessity. Been so long, that all seems idolatrous in my current, clearheaded state. Feel me?

We enjoyed the salmon and rice pilaf topped with a generous serving of whole cherry tomatoes and feta. I ate her feta, my heart issues notwithstanding. She chased my cherry tomatoes around my plate. And eventually, we got down to the numbers. She is smart, able to weigh lots of variables simultaneously. She dropped a few names of her contacts, lenders, plumbers, electricians, and others. This moved along rather quickly. And I left the conversation feeling less anxious, if not completely resolved about the issues of concern. Mostly, I now have a thought partner in Jo, which has been truly lacking as I live out these single, senior years.

On my way to Jo's office, I stopped at my favorite carwash and knocked the bird doo and tree sap off in one quick drive-through. You can count on frequent carwash errands with the large canopy of trees in most southern residential neighborhoods. I love this car wash: quick, cheap, and never out of service. So convenient on the line of East Asheville and Swannanoa, North Carolina. Good Lord, I'm home!

Driving away from Jo's downtown office, I decided to cruise by to see if the plumber's truck was gone. He was still there, not yet done replacing the drain line and reburying the pipe. My good judgment dictated that I move on without striking up a conversation. He knew what he had to do. And I was getting weary from all that talking over lunch.

Root Vegetable Stew

INGREDIENTS

20 baby carrots (4–6 inches long), whole or finely diced
3 stems of celery (not whole stalks; stems!), finely diced
2 large (fist-sized) Vidalia onions, finely diced, or cubed if you fiend for sweet onions!
5-pound bag of potatoes
1 whole chicken (deli-prepared, rotisserie chicken is a nice shortcut, if desired)
1 quart of your favorite broth can be substituted for the chicken. The marinated vegetables will deliver a tasty stew. You really can't mess this up if you tried!
Adobo seasoning, or salt and pepper to taste.

INSTRUCTIONS

Mirepoix...sometimes called the trinity, which is to say, "finely diced carrots/celery/onions." We add potatoes. And you can add chicken for a hearty winter stew, if you don't mind eating something with a face.

I prefer a slow cooker, crockpot arrangement for this dish. Pour a little olive oil in the slow cooker or crockpot, to let it heat up as you chop veggies. I usually dice up all the veggies, real fine. If you have chicken breasts, cut into meatball sized chunks. If you are taking it easy, buy a rotisserie chicken and pull the meat off the bones. That is, any bones that you don't want to eat when they are thoroughly tender and flavorful from stewing. (Just sayin'.)

MUSIC *Giving You My Problems to Work Out* by Hezekiah Walker and the Love Fellowship Choir

If using raw chicken breast chunks, allow them to cook well **before** adding the chopped veggies. If using a rotisserie chicken, cook the veggies first. When veggies are tender and the aroma encircles your head, toss in the rotisserie pieces of chicken. This stew is even better on the second day when the ingredients have become well acquainted. You can get away with leaving the stewed veggies out overnight to blend flavors. BUT be sure to refrigerate if it contains any meat stock.

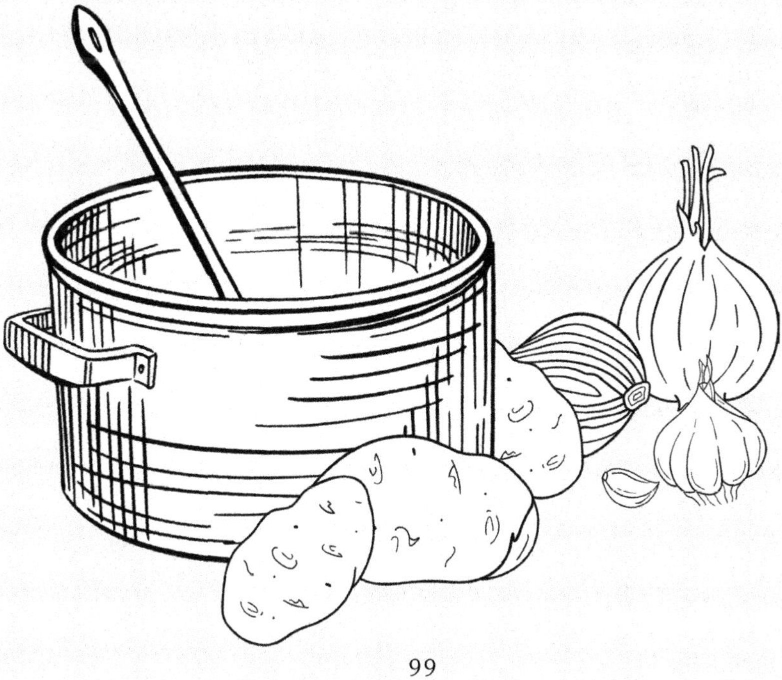

Chapter Twelve

My Baby Cousin

Getting back to my space in Black Mountain, North Carolina, I was ready for my weekly phone call with my baby girl cousin PamPam. The story of me and PamPam is a deep one, a gift rooted in our Black southern bloodline. After a separation of fifty-one years, even though we lived in neighboring states of Georgia and Alabama, my favorite aunt got us back together.

I could tell PamPam was driving when she answered. Recently widowed, PamPam does not really talk and drive. Oh, I don't know, she sometimes does answer from the car, briefly and succinctly, if it is purposeful. She answered, and I tuned in my sweetest drawl reserved for close kin, "Paa-aaamm? I can hear your car. Are you dri-iiiving, ba-aaby?" PamPam answered, "Yes, I am headed to my Georgia Sea Island resort!"

I was surprised. She was just there for a couple of weeks at Christmas, not quite a month ago. Over the Christmas holidays, she had invited me to join her. It was unworkable for me at the time, but here was another opportunity! Who said opportunity knocks but once? They lied!

I offered to meet her in south Georgia because I was in North Carolina about five hours away. She squealed with delight and shared a bit about her sudden decision as I researched the best driving routes. We were committed to making this happen. I encouraged PamPam to stop by one of her favorite Atlanta haunts, Soul Vegetarian, a restaurant in the 'hood where I was raised. I liked the image of sophisticated PamPam strolling into the restaurant in Atlanta's West End, letting her independent, metaphysical self lead the way through The Bluff to pick up whatever she needed on the road. The neighborhood was beloved by all its "alums."

Once we settled in at the resort, PamPam suggested we do a writing exercise to get reacquainted as we sat on her overstuffed sofa. She threw out as a topic: "The Old Way."

"I do not get this," I thought, "but I do not have to control everything. Let us just see where this goes."

There is a way that is ancient and vast, able to accommodate many. People often speak of the straight and narrow, but The Old Way is winding and broad. The Old Way is best followed by lanterns or lamps filled with oil. There is only One who knows the road. And it is foretold that She'll help us carry our heavy load. Yes. She's able. The Old Way is filled with righteousness, peace, and joy in the Holy Ghost. It is more than magic. It is the natural state of things. It is the pre-ordained order of life events. It is the indwelling knowledge. It is rest. The Old Way involves the engagement of mind, body, and spirit . . . and community. Something about The Old Way makes me think of the rhythm of my mama's Singer sewing machine, black and embossed with gold lettering, the kind with the wrought iron step pedal. The Old Way is tying a band tightly around the waist of a home-birthed child with a hopelessly enlarged navel after covering said navel with a Bo dollar piece for best results. Sometimes, older is better. It is pretty much always simpler.

So glad our Aunt Dot put us back together. PamPam reminds me that I am all right just as I am. We have a shared ancestral line that brings me peace and perks me up for life. She is belongingness, affirmation, warmth, and freedom, all at once. My baby cousin is a grandmother. Twice! I am at home in her love. Even with our similar eye color and sometimes persnickety ways, she knows we are who God intended us to be. Being together with PamPam is healing for me in the places where I have been so wounded. In many ways, she is my "iron that sharpens iron."

PamPam is brilliant enough and beautiful enough to not covet anybody else's beauty and brains. She is a confident woman. I love not having to be so guarded around her. She is not a hater, if you know what I mean. Truly pleased and excited about the good fortune and celebrations of others. A poultice for the soul. That's PamPam.

I am humbled before the Infinite One who knows that fifty-one years is but a moment in Eternity. God, I know that it did not have to be, this sweet reunion with my baby cousin. Thank you, God, who goes before me and has promised to be my rear guard. That's Isaiah 52:12: "For ye shall not go out with haste, nor go by flight: for the Lord will go before you; and the God of Israel will be your reward." God is always leading me and watching my back, simultaneously.

Me and PamPam turned in, knowing we would share more stories in the morning over cheesy grits and make s'mores in the evening around a firepit in the community courtyard. This was a time for "catching up," the space and context to tell every other life story to each other.

"Good morning, girl, did you sleep alright?" PamPam asked.

"Like a rock, honey! Where are we going to get coffee, this morning?" I shot back. Forgetting all about the cheesy grits, I asked about coffee before we got distracted in conversation which can be a never-ending spiral.

Out at breakfast the conversation started again. "Did you have good support when your babies were born?" she delved.

"For a little while, like three or four days. Everybody I knew had to work just to stay afloat. There was not even maternity leave, back then," I answered candidly.

"What was that like for you?" she wondered aloud.

"I was overwhelmed, child, sometimes had nightmares in those first months," I responded while allowing myself to drift back to that time.

"What do you wish could have been different? Did your husband work together with you to get through that time? Or was it supposed to be your thing, alone?"

Oh-oh, here come her multiple questions before I can get enough coffee in me to tolerate her patterns. "Fathers weren't really expected to do much, at that time. Honestly, my husband needed his sleep to keep working."

Determined to not drop this line of interrogation, PamPam continued, "Did other mothers judge and target you as a new mother, assuming you were incompetent?"

Unable to resist the invitation to complain, I promptly responded, "Oh, honey, yes! My nails were too long. My hair was not right for anybody's mother. My nursing etiquette was uncouth . . . downright 'ghetto,' as the kids like to say now. I never lost the belly fat and didn't try to suck it in. My baby cried too loud, was allergic to everything but air. I was not looking after my husband right. How could I use those tired, old, stinky cloth diapers when smart mothers were using Pampers? When was I getting back to church, and a reasonable social life? Do you even read anymore, Aubra, sugar? It was constant, I tell you, honey!" I droned on and on. She had opened that door.

I continued, how back when I was breastfeeding my firstborn, I began to understand and make all kinds of connections that were simply not a part of my conscious perceptions before then. Like when the prophet Isaiah asks, rhetorically, whether "the Lord hath forsaken me, and my Lord hath forgotten me" (49:14), God responds with another question. My and PamPam's granddaddy in common was the Baptist pastor of my family's small town in Alabama, so it is not unusual for us to strike up a conversation that is sprinkled with biblical references, advance the subject in metaphor, and then culminate into an emphatic, animated sermonic moment. Why am I trying to talk with her about God's response to Isaiah? I lost her about twenty minutes ago.

I thought this was a good time to share what I had been hearing from the Lord during my new-mother experiences: So, Pam, this is what God is revealing to me. God spoke through Isaiah, "Can a woman forget her suckling child, that she should not have compassion on the fruit of her womb?" Can a nursing mother forget her infant? This second question is followed by God's declaration, "Yes, they may forget, but I won't forget you." This is the assurance that God offers in this passage through the prophet Isaiah. God reminds us by offering a "stretch-out" comfort in these words.

Just like a breastfeeding mother experiences surges of hormones. I understand that prolactin is the milk-maker. And that oxytocin is the milk-giver. These two, prolactin and oxytocin, work together in a rhythm, making and giving our first nutrition to sustain a healthy human being. Don't interrupt me, honey, I *aaam* getting to the point. PamPam, stay with me, young'un! She asks all these compound questions with no attention to hear the complex answers. Fifty-one years of ground to cover. Good Lord, I'm home!

Cheesy Grits

Sometimes known as Grits au Gratin or Grits con Queso

INGREDIENTS

2 cups water
2 cups milk
2 cups regular grits
Sharp cheddar cheese (optional)
Chopped garlic (optional)
Parmesan cheese (optional)
Paprika (optional)
Salt to taste

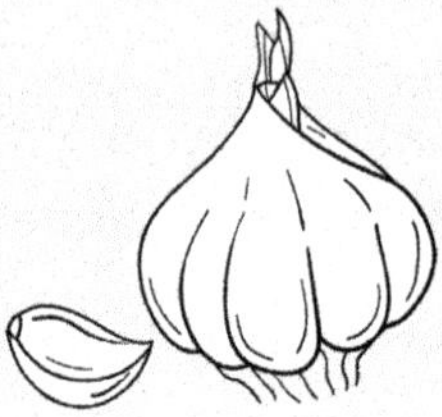

INSTRUCTIONS

Making good grits is simple as A, B, C:

A. Boil 2 cups of water, 2 cups of milk and a teensy bit of salt to your taste.
B. A little bit at a time, pour in 2 cups regular grits. Always 2:1 with grits. Pouring slowly and stirring keeps them from being lumpy.
C. Simmer on low heat and stir occasionally for 15 minutes.

For the cheesy magic, pour your cooked grits into an oil-sprayed baking pan and top with finely chopped garlic (if you like garlic as much as I do), and grated sharp cheddar. You can top with Parmesan and paprika to pretty things up. Bake for a few minutes in a 325-degree oven, just long enough to melt the cheese. Stir it up or scoop and serve. I like the corner piece. Good for any meal, from breakfast to lunch or dinner.

MUSIC *Precious Lord, Take My Hand*
by Thomas A. Dorsey

PRAYER

O God, Giver of all life, Fulfiller of all our needs, The One who loves us, feeds us, and makes us strong. You are God of everything good that we can think or imagine. You restore us, calm us, and lead us along the Way. You are good. So good. Keeper. Sustainer. I wake with you on my heart each morning. And drift into sleep meditating on your goodness and lovingkindness, at night. There is none like You. None. Like. You. Amen.

Chapter Thirteen

Who Can Open a Kola Nut?

Every bit of ministry that we manage to do, every bit of service that we give, heals us as the giver, first. This is what it means to be the first partaker. The farmer of the good fruit is the first partaker. If I have learned anything in my commitment to ministry, it is that as I care for God's people in the area of my need, God cares for me. Makes me think about when you try to save a drowning person, their violent flailing and fearful fretting could easily be the end of both of you. When life hits you like a storm, there is a point where yielding and trusting God brings us right on in to safety. With experience, I have learned how to let God have all of it and to not attempt to mastermind what I cannot handle. I have learned not to rely on parlaying my meager reserves into a bounty, without divine anointing.

This is a spiritual practice that becomes second nature after a while. The earlier in life that we encounter turbulence, the easier it may be to engage this practice. To put it another way, as long as we have never had to trust a source greater than ourselves, we do not know the experience of being snatched from danger. We can be held and comforted by that source, while we marvel at the loving-kindness. When a time comes for us to lay down our defenses, when we notice that we are all out of remedies of our own design, and the hand of the Almighty upholds us, the joy of the experience is unspeakable!

It happens.

My relational gifts are born out of the experiences of living as a woman-child who has experienced a disproportionate share of being systemically unwelcomed. Though perhaps not what I would have chosen, this path has been a blessing in ministry, empathy, and liberation work.

After a morning worship service at my predominantly white suburban church, where I serve in Silver Spring, Maryland, a truly striking woman with skin the color of a bitter kola nut stood in the narthex with her active toddler. Purposeful is the word I would use to describe her intense expression. As a sister with locs nearly all my adult life, I appreciated that she was confident enough to be sporting her naturally coarse coiffure. Then I noticed that she was very pregnant and "carrying high," which in my reproductive folk wisdom means a girl-child will soon be joining her family.

"Hi, you visiting?" After ensuing small talk and appropriate church sloganeering, I extended my hand to her and her husband who had joined us. "I'm Aubra," I offered, speaking into her surprise. Culturally, a Black churchwoman in my season of life uses a title—something ranging from "Sister" to "Miss," and a bit more rarely "Reverend" or "Bishop," but some kind of handle on that name has to be respected. "Ifeanyi," she nodded. "Akintola," her husband beamed through his youthful smile. Charming. I repeated the names and hoped to be able to recall some facsimile of them later. Insightfully, they told me that I could address the toddler as Ayo. I thought to myself, "I can do that. That's the same sound as the acronym for internalized oppression, ("I-O"). Got it. I have surely had to talk about internalized oppression (IO) enough to remember this name."

Having actively shared in the traumatic yet joyful delivery of my old-soul granddaughter, Dylan, I made a mental note to keep this young family—with their impending childbirth—in prayer. Perhaps if I had known at the time that Ifeanyi was a medical professional, my tender matriarchal heart could have been eased somewhat. But I was recovering still from the childbirth experience that I had joined in with my daughter and my son-in-law, in which we had to work together to ameliorate the thoughtless, archaic childbirth practices and inhospitable behavior of the large medical center where they insisted upon running their discriminatory patterns and policies at us.

My daughter, Tahira, had gone a few days past her predicted due date, which resulted in her progressive birthing center of midwifery refusing to attend to the delivery and referring us to a nearby hospital. During her hospital admission, a staff person confessed that, "With a name like Goldson, I was expecting a Jew. Well, whaddya know, Tahira Goldson is a Black woman!"

This was simply a preview of what the next several hours of objectification, unresponsiveness, and subsequent verbal assaults would include. The experience was a study in the full range of antisemitism to anti-Black racism to misogynistic, coercive tactics by hospital staff and practicing professionals. As a native Southerner, rooted in my Blackness, and unaccustomed to this institutional level of such bigotry, I was quickly trying to grasp, "Who are these people? And why are they so mean and uninviting?"

I was nothing but proud of my children who handled all of this with grace, dignity, and the necessary firmness. They had studied together for this treasured experience. My daughter, as a first-time mother, was concerned about the research data she came across which reported that epidural medication can cause decreased fetal heart rate and hinder the "latch on" response for a newborn trying to breastfeed. I was given a lesson on the artificial hormone, Pitocin, and how it works to speed up the delivery process. The only problem is that it usually does not speed up cervical dilation or aid in relaxing a mother's pelvis. Sort of puts the baby in a "Ready or not, here I come!" situation with the mother bearing the brunt of this experience. I do not have to tell you that this is devastating to the mother's body, often tearing the birth canal, and traumatizing the spiritual well-being.

Many women and their babies have historically had successful childbirth experiences without so much interference. Renowned midwife Ina May Gaskin noted that most mammals give birth without much intervention; starting in the 1970s, Gaskin taught a method of childbearing that used maternal body positioning to overcome certain birthing challenges. My son-in-law and I were abandoned in the hospital room by the medical staff when my daughter refused Pitocin and anesthesia out of her commitment to natural childbirth. My daughter simply did not want to emerge from this experience with ruptured reproductive organs and a baby who was dizzy drunk from the epidural anesthesia. Tahira was making hard and excellent choices about her body and that of her unborn daughter. I shudder when I think of what kind of love helps someone to make such a physically painful and brave choice to hold on for the best outcomes in this sacrificial way. That girl, Tahira, is something else. I love every breath she breathes!

We were left totally alone, after being admonished by medical staff to not dim the lights in the room as my daughter tried to relax into advancing labor pains. They were angry that these Black folk, a girl from Georgia and a boy from Jamaica, had the audacity to research, study, and make choices about her body . . . and to show up with a mother in tow who was unable to speak but who reminded them of how much they were loved. There we were—my daughter, son-in-law, and me—in the bathroom adjoining the patient room of this state-of-the-art medical facility. Our crowning baby girl, sunny side up, was coming into the world with a puzzled, excited look in her brand-new eyes!

I could not vocally advocate for my daughter during this childbirth event, as I was still unable to speak. You know, God worked mightily through my son-in-law and his very direct, matter-of-fact communication with the hospital staff, while endowing me with gentleness and stability for Tahira. By grace, we got through it. Exhausted, we took turns shaking, crying, and sleeping. I dozed in the broad windowsills of the hospital room, while Tahira and Dylan slept nearby in the bed. No cots or rollaway beds offered. To describe it as traumatizing would be an understatement.

But we got through it. I am reminded of the commitment of Shadrach, Meshach, and Abednego clinging steadfastly to the God who brought them through past trials. "Did not we cast three [people] bound into the midst of the fire?" asks King Nebuchadnezzar, when he sees four people "walking in the midst of the fire, and they have no hurt; and the form of the fourth looks like God" (Daniel 3:24–25). We, all three, were intact. And our new fourth one truly looks like God! It is well.

If you need to be reminded of how good God is, let me tell you that last summer, Dylan was awarded from her local library in Crofton, Maryland, the distinction of "One Thousand Books Before Kindergarten." And my determined, compassionate daughter launched a thriving home health business that delivers a myriad of non-medical services to post-surgical discharge patients, new mothers, seniors who choose to age in place, and anyone who needs care and advocacy as they go through times of diminished capacity. Not everyone has close family support. There must be a reliable place to seek this accompaniment that we will all need at some point. Only months after giving birth, she saw me through a medial thyroplasty surgery to restore my ability to make vocal sounds—to talk, preach, and sing—and to drink liquids after eating solid foods; to draw a full breath, to hold it, and release as I paced my exertion in Yoga, Zumba, dance, and other long-abandoned bodily pleasures.

At the birth of Ifeanyi's baby girl, I was free (in terms of bandwidth) to pray for their family . . . for Ifeanyi and Akintola, for Ayo and their new baby girl. During our planning of the baptism of these daughters, I was nudged by the Holy Spirit to offer to officiate a traditional naming ceremony, drawing on my West African ministry experience.

One of the most profound experiences of my life in ministry was being immersed in African traditional religion in West Africa. I understood and embraced so much more of myself than I would have imagined possible. I served a post in the Pan-African Christian Conference, organized by the late and most honorable, beloved Dr. Ndugu T'Ofori-Atta—my seminary professor who was still having babies when most men his age were struggling to divest themselves of the bitterness that had accumulated over a life of brutal marginalization. He was earnestly loving with his adult children, his wife and newborn, and a host of friends, family, and seminary disciples. May peace rest upon his sweet soul.

I was prepared and full of zeal to celebrate Ifeanyi's daughters in a naming ceremony. We can thank Dr. T'Ofori-Atta and my extended time of leading worship in West Africa. My experiences there moved me from deep grief over my mother's death to an infinite connection to my mother, grandmother, and great-grandmother, to enhanced gratitude for my adult children and grandchild. Each act of healing that we extend reciprocally heals each of us, too. That's just how it works.

Being clear that our white, suburban congregation could not manage the multiple-day tradition or all-night dancing that might occur at a typical naming ceremony in their ancestral Nigeria, I sought consent from the young couple to proceed with a modified coffee-hour version of this celebration. Ifeanyi endorsed the idea with an enthusiastic smile, "Come through, Rev. Aubra! Come through!"

I was confident that I could adorn the newly renovated church social hall in authentic West African textiles from my own personal travel collection. Our music ministry had shelves of percussive gourd-like instruments, and our grown-women's circle, "Sisters for Sisters," knows how to throw a potluck and lead with a kindhearted atmosphere. Our ninety-eight-year-old grand-lady founder of "Sisters for Sisters" with the jade-colored, smiling eyes, is June

Leonard. I love being near enough to June in the sanctuary to hear her strong, youthful singing voice. Retiring from the choir many years ago, her melodious voice still bellows around the sanctuary. The "Sisters" are a warm, agenda-less group that gathers monthly for healing conversation, laughter, food, and sometimes the simple bearing of griefs and disappointments. Any woman in the church can show up on the third Sunday with or without a potluck dish to reconnect to our sisterhood of faith, share yearnings and aspirations, or to wallow in disappointment. Joan Boyer supports Lady June in many tasks; June has a vision but lacks sufficient energy to implement. We all pitch in and the men of the church drop by for a slice of something or a refreshing drink.

Pastor Matt welcomed the extended family and friends of Akintola and Ifeanyi who showed up in large numbers, attired in elegant, traditional ceremonial garments. A veritable feast for the eyes with rich colors of fabric and skin tones, an assortment of tapestries and brocades, and so much glorious textured hair, all characterized by warm, dignified mingling.

This was a few months before the local county commissioners considered the "CROWN Act" to ban discrimination against natural hair of African-heritage persons, especially in the workplace. Our hair was about to be declared "Free!" after years of our hair's resistance against discrimination and insistence to show its true nature in all types of settings—from swimming pools to commercial kitchens, to service work, to any vigorous activity that sweated out the effects of a perm or hot comb. The crown was finally winning its battle for welcome in respectable, public places. My, my, my!

I was filled to overflowing while beholding such beauty, openness, and warmth in this naming ceremony! Later, I would recall that the ambience was much like the church of my formative years where everyone was family by blood or by circumstance. At this naming ceremony, Good Lord, I knew I was home!

I opened our celebration with a brief twelve-step reading to remind us that nothing worthwhile was ever accomplished without enthusiasm. I offered, "For my own health and recovery, and for that of my fellows, it is useful to remain mindful that our most unhealthy compulsions never take a day off. This poor impulse control will often use celebration as an opportunity to embolden itself. So, lay aside your impulses, urges, and burdens, and allow yourself to experience this as a fresh moment in your worship encounters. We are blessed to be the great cloud of witnesses in this naming ceremony."

Several parishioners were prearranged to offer the family one of seven key elements to honor and bless the names of their young daughters. Gathered congregants bestowed blessings on the family while detailing the meanings of each element. These blessings were preprinted on small cue cards to support the confidence of our mostly white, suburban congregation whose hearts yearn for inclusively welcoming all who seek a church-home. Because the cultural iterations within the beautiful Nigerian rituals can vary greatly, we were granted broad latitude for a liturgy offered by our congregation.

A Nigerian child's naming ceremony may use different types of food materials, including water, kola nut, palm oil, salt, alligator pepper, bitter cola, wine, and honey. Realizing that I had not a clue as to how to open a kola nut, at this point in the ceremony, I posed the question to the seating area of the grandparents. Looking on their faces, I was reminded of the women of my maternal family who were all lively and engaging scholars devoted to early childhood education and rectifying the impact of systemic racism on the early years of development. My mother's features and voice cadence were distinctly West African. She had a generous gap in her front teeth and dark brown skin with strong, agile hands that could open the toughest Brazil nut while simultaneously plaiting hair and dressing it with olive oil or sweet-smelling pomades. Her memory swelled in my heart nearly beyond speech. Remembering that my mother was "just more," I searched the grandparents and entreated a volunteer, "Who can open a kola nut?"

Ifeanyi, eager to ease the moment, quickly responded with a daughter's pride, "Daddy?" . . . as if to say, "Surely this is a job for you." Her father took the kola nut from my hand, offered up a quick smile, and placed the nut in the open hands of Akintola's father. The act was akin to saying, "I place my daughter and granddaughters in your hands, with full assurance that you will care for them in the most loving and appropriate manner." All that in one gesture. "I am trusting you with this moment and the next." Akintola's father received the kola nut, appeared to slide one spirited thumbnail across it, and returned the meat of the nut to my hand with a nod of approval that silently said, "Go ahead." I was relieved and grateful that the family patriarchs understood my less-than-perfect display of compassion and celebration.

This moment was so full for me. No dream-killing competition for attention, no machismo and performance anxiety, and no grandstanding. Just freely giving what the moment required. I was too through!

There is something so sweet and healing about cooperation, mutual respect, and demonstrative love among communities, among families. That mutual respect and demonstrative love was saturating our church social hall as the sacred naming ceremony was taking place. As the organizer and celebrant, I may have needed it more than anyone.

We sealed the time by joyously dancing to Sammie Okposo's "Jehovah Done Do Me Something." (It is a marvelous ting, O!) I had been forewarned by church leadership that our church—a maturing upscale predominantly white congregation, located outside the Chocolate City of Washington, DC—may feel uncomfortable with any dancing. I think affluent, old white people like to have a good time, too! In order to address any reluctance to dance, I placed baskets of white hand towels near each seating area. "For anyone who believes that they cannot dance, a fresh hand towel waived overhead in a circular motion can provide similar gratification and nearly as much jubilance as spontaneous dance." As my good-humored preaching uncles often said when they were about to impart some commonsense counsel, "I'm going to tell you this, free of charge!"

One of our white congregants, the eighty-three-year-old Dr. David Smock, whose daughters were born in Ghana, "raised the roof" with the palms of his hands bouncing toward the ceiling. During my planning, Dr. Smock shared his enthusiasm by divulging that his daughters had a naming ceremony in Ghana.

Estelle Franklin, originally from New Orleans, did a mean second-line dance, towel waving overhead, that was totally fit for the hottest Mardi Gras festival. Lord Jesus, Estelle! Let's do that cakewalk, "Oh when the Saints go marchin' in!"

Pastor Gloria graced us with her version of a Caribbean whining dance, holy of course. Lord! Lord!

"First Lady" Christy Braddock cleared her own space with fun-girl moves and a spinning towel on alternate sides. Work it, Ms. Chris! Don't hurt nobody!

The guests of honor, Akintola and Ifeanyi, their toddler, infant, and the godparents, danced about with glee. Oh, clear the floor for that irresistible Shoki dancing! Nigeria all up in the house!

Even my frequently cautious granddaughter, Dylan, now four years old, lost her careful restraint, grabbing Pastor Matt around his knees, getting lost in the billows of his ample white clergy robe. Trying to keep his balance, he reached for her in the fabric. Completely uncooperative, Dylan convulsed with laughter as he attempted to free her (and himself) from the full skirt of the robe. Tangled in the billows, Dylan spun and giggled until she dizzily fell out of the fabric, with roaring laughter.

My daughter, Tahira, swayed with me in a dance, preserving just enough energy to help restore the order of the social hall, gather my artifacts, mud cloth, kente fabric, holy vessels, instruments, baskets, and all altar items. What would I do without my daughter? I mean, really.

The redemptive healing and love left many of us soul-satisfied and affirmed our new members, Akintola and Ifeanyi, and their place among us.

I was a long way from my own homebirth in the Jim Crow South, where being Black was viewed as a pathology. I was celebrating an extended West African family who had come to North America in freedom, by choice. We were in my white suburban church, with two Black baby girls who, hopefully, will never know the institutional rejection, physical brutality, and spiritual assault of the baby girls of West African ancestry who were stolen from their homeland and brought to this country in shackles and chains—forced to lie in their own excrement on a cruise of cruelty to a new world that promised only suffering, separation from loved ones, and hundreds of years of forced labor. God has promised to never forget us. While we struggle and await the restorative justice of basic civility and economic reparations, our lactating God is the embodied amen and has not forgotten.

As the church, we make this manifest through liturgy, worship, and sacred ritual, activism and healing all that is broken. We are made a little more whole in this unlikely place where God still manages to come through long enough to heal, restore, renew, revitalize, and remember. "Come through, God. Come through!"

Jollof Rice

BODY BREAK

MUSIC *A Marvelous Thing* by Sammie Okposo

I've heard it said that every culture has its own rice recipe. It's fundamental.

INGREDIENTS

3¾ cups (750g) long grain parboiled rice
2–3 cups stewed tomatoes
1 chicken (whole chicken, drumsticks or chicken breast)
2 medium Vidalia onions (if in season)
1 clove garlic
chilis, to taste
ginger, to taste (FRESH)
3 Knorr cubes (maybe you call this "chicken bouillon")
2 teaspoons thyme
2 teaspoons curry powder (Nigerian curry powder)
pepper and salt (to taste)
palm oil (or olive oil)

INSTRUCTIONS

Prepare the tomato stew first, so everything has time to blend while making the rice.

Sauté onions, garlic, chilis, ginger in palm oil (you could use olive oil, but palm oil makes it red in color). Once you have sautéed the onions, garlic and chilis until those onions appear to be clear, like you can see through them, then add stewed tomatoes. This is when you put in your seasonings to suit your taste.

Do not overcook. The aroma of this will saunter through your nostrils, making your mouth water and your tastebuds stand at attention!

If you are all about flavor, let this mixture ripen overnight before adding the rice. Because, see, your rice is going to taste like everything you put in that mix. The blend is our defining factor.

Ready to cook the rice. Some prefer to wash their rice for less starchy, sometimes stuck together grains. Personally, I like all the minerals, starchy, stuck-togetherness of my rice. To each her own, child!

Put in the rice, stir. Add some water, stir, and cook for 2–3 minutes to cook off the water. The rice will drink it right up. Add your tomato concoction and stir together. Cover the whole thing and let it rest on low heat for about 15 minutes. Turn off the low heat and let the dish stand for 5 more minutes, take the lid off and fluff your jollof rice. Ummm, perfect!

PRAYER

Spirit of Breakthrough! Spirit of Peace! We call on you to release all your mighty and consistent Power in this new season and have your way such that all will know you've come through blessing with wisdom and compassion. Show yourself strong. Show yourself loving. Make your manifold wisdom apparent. We love you, God, with our whole selves . . . our hearts, our souls, our minds, our bodies, and even those facets of ourselves that are yet unnamed. We love you with everything that we are, known and unknown.